Learn AutoCAD® 12
in a Day

Ralph Grabowski

Wordware Publishing, Inc.

Library of Congress Cataloging-in-Publication Data

Grabowski, Ralph
    Learn AutoCAD 12 in a Day / by Ralph Grabowski
      p.   cm.
    Includes index.
    ISBN 1-55622-339-0
    1. Computer graphics.   2. AutoCAD (Computer graphics).
    I. Title.
    T385.G69243   1993
    620'.0042'02855369--dc20   92-43323
                                            CIP

ISBN1-55622-339-0

10 9 8 7 6 5 4 3 2 1

9212

AutoCAD is a registered trademark of Autodesk, Inc.
Other product names mentioned are used for identification purposes only and may be
trademarks of their respective companies.

All inquiries for volume purchases of this book should be addressed to
Wordware Publishing, Inc., at the above address. Telephone inquiries may be
made by calling:

(214) 423-0090

Contents

PART I
TWO-DIMENSIONAL DRAFTING

HOUR ONE

SETTING UP THE DRAWING

INTRODUCTION

In this chapter, you learn how to start AutoCAD Release 12 and set it up in preparation for drawing. You tour the AutoCAD user interface and get your feet wet by drawing a few lines. By the end of the chapter, you know how to save your work to disk and how to get out of AutoCAD.

BEFORE YOU BEGIN

To learn AutoCAD in a day, you work with a drawing based on something you can easily find: the yard. The example used for the two-dimensional drafting portion of this book creates and modifies a drawing of the yard around your home.

Before you begin this tutorial, you may want to measure your yard and locate major features, such as the house, driveway, and garden areas.

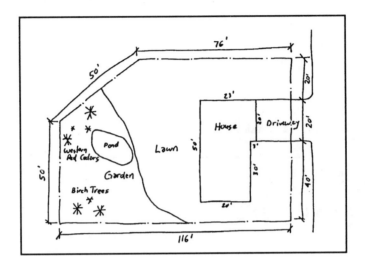

If you'd rather not or if your home doesn't have a yard, you can follow along with the yard sketch above, which is the drawing this book uses.

STARTING AUTOCAD

When the installation program installed AutoCAD on your computer, it created a DOS batch file called ACADR12.BAT. (If AutoCAD is not yet installed on your computer, read Appendix A, Installing and Configuring AutoCAD.) Running the batch file starts AutoCAD.

At the DOS prompt, type the following:

```
C:\> acadr12 <Enter>
```

Pressing <Enter> runs the batch file, which sets some DOS environment variables and then automatically loads AutoCAD. Depending on the speed of your computer, it takes between 20 seconds to more than a minute to load AutoCAD. While AutoCAD loads, the copyright notice briefly appears.

```
                 A U T O C A D (R)
   Copyright (c) 1982-92 Autodesk, Inc. All Rights Reserved.
   Release 12 (6/21/92) 386 DOS Extender
   Serial Number:  117-100000000
   Licensed to:    Ralph Grabowski
   Obtained from:  Autodesk, Inc - (415) 332-2344
```

Then the screen switches to graphics mode and displays the Autodesk logo.

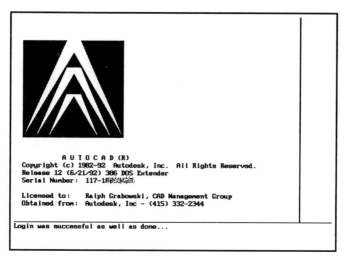

THE DRAWING EDITOR

When the Drawing Editor appears, it consists of a graphical drawing area surrounded on three sides by text areas: the status line, the side screen menu, and the command prompt area.

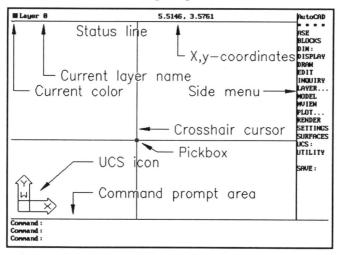

THE STATUS LINE At the top of the Drawing Editor is the status line, which reports information on the current state of the drawing. From left to right, the status line tells you:

- the current color, white
- the current layer name, as in "Layer 0"
- whether ortho, snap, or paper space modes are set, as in "Ortho Snap P"
- the current x,y-coordinates, as in "5.5146, 3.5761"

You can see how the status line displays settings by turning on the ortho mode, as follows:

1. Press function key <F8>.
2. Notice the word "Ortho" on the status line.
3. Press <F8> again to turn off ortho mode. The word Ortho disappears from the status line.

THE SIDE SCREEN MENU Along the right side is the screen menu. It lets you enter a command by picking the name from a list. The menu supplied with AutoCAD groups commands together in logical order. For example, all display-related commands appear in the Display submenu.

Try using the screen menu right now:

1. Move your pointing device (the mouse or tablet puck or tablet stylus) to the right until a highlight bar appears on the screen menu.
2. Move the pointing device up or down until the word **Display** is highlighted.
3. Press the first button (the leftmost button on a mouse; the tip button on the stylus) to select the Display submenu. Instantly, a new menu appears that lists AutoCAD's display options.
4. Now select the **REDRAW:** item to execute the Redraw command. The graphics screen blinks as AutoCAD redraws the screen.
5. To return to the first menu, move the highlight bar to **AutoCAD** at the top and press the pick button again.

THE COMMAND AREA Along the bottom is the command prompt area. Here you type AutoCAD commands. Here is where

AutoCAD prompts you for additional information it might need to complete the command. When you see Command prompt:

```
Command:
```

it means AutoCAD is ready for you to type a command name. Try drawing a few lines now:

1. Type the Line command, as follows:
   ```
   Command: line <Enter>
   ```

Type the word LINE, then press the <Enter> key.

2. The prompt changes from "Command:" to "From point:."
   ```
   From point:
   ```

AutoCAD is asking you where the line should start from. As you move the pointing device, you see the cross hair cursor move about the drawing portion of the screen.

3. Pick a point on the screen by pressing the first button (also known as the "pick button") on your pointing device. AutoCAD changes the prompt to read
   ```
   To point:
   ```

   and a "rubber band" line stretches from the point you picked as you move the pointing device around.

4. Move the pointing device some more and press the pick button again. You have drawn your first line in AutoCAD!

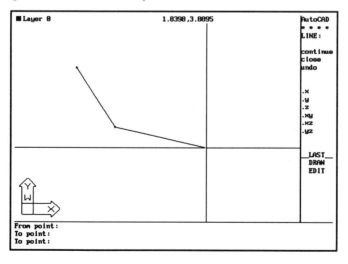

5. Draw another line by moving the pointing device and pressing the pick button.

6. You end the Line command by pressing the <Enter> key, or pressing <Ctrl>-C, or pressing the second button (the rightmost mouse button; the barrel button on the stylus), as follows:

```
To point: <Enter>
```

7. To erase the lines you drew, type U and press <Enter> at the command prompt to undo the lines you drew, as follows:

```
Command: u
line
```

THE TEXT SCREEN   If you need to see more than three lines of the command prompt area, you can switch to the text screen by pressing function key <F1>. Instantly, the graphics screen is replaced by a text screen displaying the 24 most recent lines of text.

You return to the graphics screen by pressing <F1> again. Function key <F1> is called the "flipscreen" key.

THE CROSS HAIR CURSOR   As you saw while drawing the line, the cross hair cursor shows where you are in the drawing. The small box in the center of the cross hairs is called the "pickbox." When you select an object in the drawing, the pickbox shows you the point you are picking. You use the pickbox in Hour 4, Changing the Landscape.

THE UCS ICON   Now that you have some experience with the drawing area, there is one other feature worth pointing out. The UCS icon (UCS is short for "user coordinate system") is in the lower left corner. The icon shows the direction of the x- and y-axes. The icon is primarily used for orienting yourself in three-dimensional drafting (see Part Two, Three-Dimensional Design).

If you find the icon getting in the way, you can turn it off with the Ucsicon command, as follows:

```
Command: ucsicon
ON/OFF/All/Noorigin/ORigin/<ON>: off
```

Now that you are familiar with the AutoCAD drawing screen, you can go ahead and set up the drawing environment.

PREPARING FOR DRAWING THE YARD

Before you draw the yard, you need to prepare AutoCAD for a new drawing. For the remainder of this first hour, you learn how to name the drawing, set the units, snap, and grid, turn on the coordinate display, set the limits, and name the layers.

NAME THE DRAWING   To give a new drawing a filename, use the Saveas command as follows:

Command: **saveas**

AutoCAD displays a dialog box called Save Drawing As.

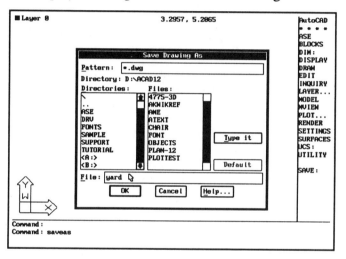

This dialog box has several areas that you get to by picking buttons and lists with your mouse or the <Tab> key:

- At the top of the dialog box is the Pattern: text entry box, which is currently set to "*.dwg." This is a filter that specifies which files are displayed by this dialog box.
- The Directories: list box lists the names of subdirectories in the current directory. By double clicking on a subdirectory, you change to that subdirectory. Double clicking on "ACAD" moves you directly to the AutoCAD directory.
- The Files: list box lists the DWG drawing files in the current subdirectory.

- The File: text entry box is where you type in the new name for the drawing. Call the drawing "yard," as follows:

```
File: yard
Current drawing name set to D:\ACAD\YARD.
```

After you press <Enter>, AutoCAD saves the drawing in the current subdirectory with the name YARD.DWG. and removes the dialog box. From now on, you and AutoCAD refer to this drawing as "Yard."

At the bottom of all dialog boxes are three buttons:

- **OK** exits the dialog box with the changes you made.
- **Cancel** exits the dialog box and discards the changes you made.
- **Help...** brings up a second dialog box with helpful information on using the current dialog box or command.

If you prefer not to use the dialog box, click on "Type it." AutoCAD removes the dialog box and displays the following prompt:

```
Save current changes as:
```

Here, enter the name "Yard" and press <Enter>.

SETTING THE UNITS AutoCAD can work with a variety of measurement styles, such as fractional, decimal, and exponential. Once you set a measurement style with the Ddunits command, AutoCAD expects to read all input in that style; AutoCAD also displays all measurements in that style of units.

AutoCAD does not work in metric or imperial units. Rather, it simply works in unitless units and leaves it to you to interpret what the units mean.

The Ddunits command allows you to set the type of measurement and orientation of angular measurement.

1. Type the Ddunits command at the Command: prompt, as follows:
```
Command: ddunits
```

AutoCAD displays the Units Control dialog box.

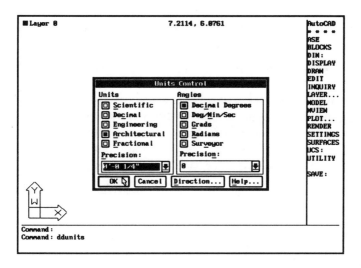

2. On the left are the five forms of units AutoCAD works with. When you measured your yard, you probably measured the distances in feet, inches, and fractional inches. For this reason, you should pick the box next to **Architectural**. If you measured your yard in meters and centimeters, you would pick the box next to Decimal.

3. Below Units is the **Precision** list box. Measurements to the nearest 1/4-inch are accurate enough for this project. Click on the down arrow and select the 0'-0 1/4" item. You can still enter distances more accurately than 1/4-inch because AutoCAD remembers distances to full accuracy. However, AutoCAD will display coordinates and distances to the nearest 1/4".

4. The Ddunits command also controls the display and orientation of angles and bearings in a drawing. On the right of the dialog box are the five kinds of angles AutoCAD works with. By default, AutoCAD uses the Cartesian method of measuring angles:

   • Fractional degrees are measured in decimals.
   • 0 degrees is to the East (the positive x-direction).
   • Positive angles are measured counterclockwise.

If we were real land surveyors, we would use the Ddunits command to change fractional degrees to minutes and seconds. The **Direction...** button brings up a second dialog box that lets you change the 0-degree orientation to North and measure positive angles clockwise. However,

AutoCAD's method of angle measurement is so pervasive that we will retain the default values for the purpose of learning AutoCAD in a day.

5. When you finish setting the units, pick the **OK** button.

TURNING ON COORDINATES, SNAP, AND GRID In a new drawing, AutoCAD continuously displays updated coordinates on the status line. (In releases of AutoCAD previous to Release 12, coordinates did not display because the continuous display of coordinates slowed down older, slower computers.)

1. To turn the coordinate display off, press function key <F6>, as follows:

    ```
    Command: <F6> <Coords off>
    ```

AutoCAD responds with the message "<Coords off>" to confirm that it has turned off the continuous display of coordinates. Press <F6> again to turn coordinates back on:

```
Command: <F6> <Coords on>
```

2. When you move the pointing device around, you see the value of the x,y-coordinates rapidly changing.

One great advantage to drawing with a computer is that it allows you to create very accurate drawings. AutoCAD has several features that help you draw with perfect accuracy. One is called "snap" mode; you learn about others later in the book. AutoCAD's snap can be thought of as setting a drawing resolution.

3. To draw everything to an accuracy of one inch, use the Snap command as follows:

    ```
    Command: snap
    Snap spacing or ON/OFF/Aspect/Rotate/Style <0'- 1">: on
    ```

4. Move your pointing device around and note how the cursor jumps on the screen instead of moving smoothly. The cursor is jumping in one-inch increments. Look at the coordinate display and notice it is changing by the nearest inch, rather than the nearest quarter-inch as set by the Ddunits command.

5. As a visual guide, turn on a grid (an array of dots) with the Grid command, as follows:

    ```
    Command: grid
    Grid spacing(X) or ON/OFF/Snap/Aspect <0'-0">: 1"
    ```

The array of dots appears, spaced one inch apart.

6. A fine grid clutters up the screen. After all, the grid is meant to guide you—not to get in your way. Now change the spacing to 10 feet, as follows:

```
Command: <Enter>
Grid spacing(X) or ON/OFF/Snap/Aspect <1'-0">: 10'
```

By pressing the <Enter> key at the Command: prompt, you repeat the previous command, the Grid command in this case. This AutoCAD feature lets you quickly repeat the command several times over.

The grid disappears when you set the grid spacing to ten feet—don't worry, we bring it back later.

SETTING THE LIMITS There is no practical limit to the size of drawing you can create with AutoCAD. You could draw the entire solar system full-size if you wanted. The Limits command is useful for showing the nominal limits of a drawing and for constraining the limits of the grid marks. By specifying the lower left and upper right coordinates, you constrain the limits of the grid marks and the display of the Zoom All command.

Take a look at the sketch of your yard. Leaving about 20 feet of "breathing room" around the edges of the example drawing, work out the dimensions of the limits. Assume that the lower left corner of the yard is located at (0,0).

1. Type the Limits command and enter the coordinates of the lower left and upper right corners, as follows:

```
Command: limits
Reset Model space limits:
ON/OFF/<Lower left corner> <0'-0",0'-0">: -20',-20'
Upper right corner <1'-0",0'-9">: 140',100'
```

2. Now use the Zoom All command to see the extents of the drawing limits, as follows:

```
Command: zoom
All/Center/Dynamic/Extents/Left/Previous/Vmax/Window/
    <Scale(X/XP)>: a
Regenerating drawing.
```

For most of AutoCAD's command options, you only need to type the first letter of the option. Here you type "a" as the abbreviation for the "All" option.

The grid dots reappear as AutoCAD displays the larger area. Previously, AutoCAD displayed an area one foot by nine inches; now

AutoCAD displays 160 feet by 120 feet. Thus, the zoom command lets you see the "big picture" as well as zooming in for a detailed look.

CREATING NEW LAYERS If you have worked with overlay drafting, then you are familiar with the concept of layers. In overlay drafting, you draw the base plan on one mylar sheet, the electrical on another sheet, and the structural on a third. Since the mylar is transparent, you can overlay the three drawings to create a single blueprint.

Layers in CAD operate in a similar manner. You draw parts of the drawing on different layers. Then, you turn layers off and on to display the drawing in different ways. For example, the electrical contractor might be interested in seeing only the base plan layer and the electrical layer.

AutoCAD lets you use layer names up to 31 characters long, effectively giving you an unlimited number of layers in a drawing.

Until now, you have been typing AutoCAD's commands at the Command: prompt. Typing the full command names is a fast way to draw and edit if you are a touch typist, but it is slow if you aren't. As mentioned earlier in this chapter, AutoCAD has several different ways to let you enter commands. The easiest way to set up layer names is with AutoCAD's pop-down menus.

1. Move your pointing device up to the status line. As you do, you see the status line change into a "menu bar." Simultaneously, the cross hair cursor changes into a pointer cursor.

2. Move the pointer cursor until the word "Settings" is highlighted.

3. When you press the pick button on your pointing device, the Settings menu pops down.

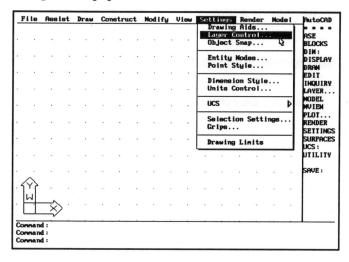

4. Use your pointing device to move the pointer cursor down until the line "Layer Control..." is highlighted.

5. Press the pick button again; the Layer Control dialog box appears. The dialog box lets you control almost every aspect of AutoCAD's layers. As you can see, the only layer currently in the drawing is a layer called "0." Every new AutoCAD drawing has this one layer.

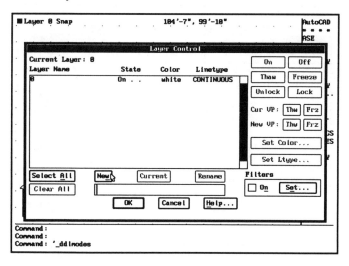

6. Create a layer by typing the first layer name, Lot, in the text box across from the **Clear All** button. Pick the **New** button to add Lot to the list of layer names.

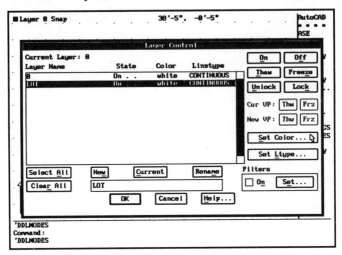

7. If you have a color display, you may want to assign a color to each layer. This makes it easy to determine which lines belong to which layer. Change the color of the Lot layer to blue by picking layer name Lot, then the **Set Color...** button (located on the right side of the dialog box). A second dialog box appears, called Select Color.

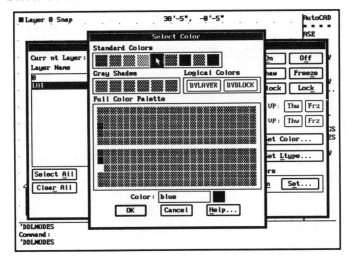

8. The Select Color dialog box displays either 16 or 256 colors, depending on the capabilities of your computer's graphics board. Pick the blue box at the top of the dialog box. The word "Blue" appears next the Color text box at the bottom of the dialog box.

9. Pick the **OK** button to exit the Select Color dialog box. The name of the color next to layer Lot changes to "blue."

10. Add the remaining layer names and colors, using the following table as a guide:

Layer Name	Layer Color
House	white
Road	red
Lawn	magenta (pink)
Plants	green
Pond	cyan (light blue)

11. When you finish, pick the Lot layer name, then the **Current** button. All drawing from now on occurs on the Lot layer.

12. To exit the Layer Control dialog box, pick **OK** button at the bottom of the dialog box.

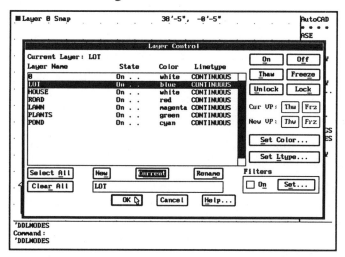

SAVING THE DRAWING (Save, Savetime, Quit)

Let's review the drawing to this point. Although you haven't drawn anything yet, the drawing file contains a fair amount of information.

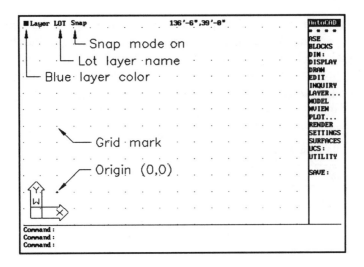

On the status line, you can see the color of the current layer is blue and its name is Lot. You also see that snap mode is turned on, that the coordinates are displaying in feet and inches, and the grid is turned on. The figure above also shows you where the origin (0,0) is located. In the next chapter, you begin drawing the lot from the origin.

For speed, AutoCAD keeps the drawing in the computer's memory. The drawback is that if the computer crashes or if the power is cut, you lose your work. Although crashes and power outages are not common, it is still a good idea to save your drawing every ten or fifteen minutes.

You save your drawing to disk with the Save command, as follows:

1. Type the Save command:
   ```
   Command: save
   ```

A dialog box appears on the screen that looks the same as the Saveas command's dialog box. Pick the OK button to save the drawing to disk.

2. Release 12 lets you set a time to automatically save the drawing, without using the Save command. The default setting, 120 minutes, is far too infrequent to do any good. Decrease the automatic save time to every 15 minutes, as follows:
   ```
   Command: savetime
   New value for SAVETIME <120>: 15
   ```

AutoCAD will save the drawing to file AUTO.SV$ every fifteen minutes. If you are using an AutoCAD command, AutoCAD waits until the command ends before performing the automatic save:

```
Command:
Automatic save to C:\auto.sv$ ...
Command:
```

Even though AutoCAD saves the drawing automatically, it is still a good idea to save your work after finishing a lot of work.

3. If you need to take a break at this point, use the Quit command to leave the Drawing Editor, as follows:

```
Command: quit
End AutoCAD.
C:\ACAD>
```

You exit AutoCAD and you find yourself back at the DOS prompt.

In the next chapter, you begin drawing the yard with AutoCAD based on the sketch you created earlier—or based on the example given in this book. You also learn how to make simple changes and print out a copy of the drawing on your printer.

HOUR TWO

DRAWING THE YARD OUTLINE

INTRODUCTION

In the first hour, you learned how to start AutoCAD, set up a new drawing, and save the drawing to the computer's hard disk. This hour, you learn how to draw accurate lines, make simple changes to the drawing, and produce a copy of the drawing on your printer.

BRINGING BACK THE YARD DRAWING (Open)

If you exited AutoCAD at the end of the last hour, you need to reload AutoCAD and the Yard drawing.

1. Load AutoCAD with the ACADR12.BAT batch file, as follows:

   ```
   C:\> acadr12
   ```

2. When AutoCAD's Drawing Editor appears, type the Open command, as follows:

   ```
   Command: open
   ```

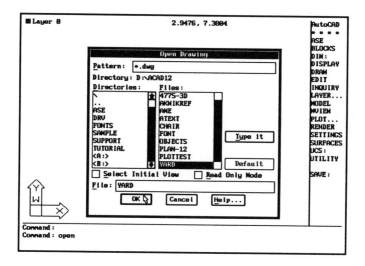

3. When the dialog box appears, look for the text cursor (the vertical line) flashing in the text box next to **File:**.

4. Type the name **yard**.

5. Press <Enter> to exit the dialog box.

AutoCAD loads the yard drawing and displays it on the screen. It should look exactly the same as when you last saw the drawing.

DRAWING THE LOT BOUNDARY (Line)

Let's get some lines on the screen! To orient yourself, the first thing you should draw is the boundary of the yard. The lines making up the lot boundary are drawn with the Line command.

1. Begin drawing the lot lines at the lower left corner, the origin (0,0), as follows:
   ```
   Command: line
   From point: 0,0
   ```

2. To draw the lower 116'-long boundary line, you know that the other end of the line must be located at coordinate (116',0):
   ```
   To point: 116',0
   ```

3. The next line is 80 feet north, which is coordinate (116',80'):
   ```
   To point: 116',80'
   ```

4. You drew the first two lines with absolute coordinates, where you calculated the coordinates based on your measurements.

However, AutoCAD can do the calculations for you. When you use "relative coordinates," AutoCAD draws a line from the current point based on the length and direction you specify. Continue drawing the lot boundary using relative coordinates, as follows:

```
To point: @76'<180
To point: @50'<216.88
```

When you tell AutoCAD to draw a line with relative coordinates, you use a special notation that has the following meaning:

Notation	Meaning
@	Use relative coordinates
76'	Distance is 76 feet from the previous end point
<	Draw the line at an angle...
180	...of 180 degrees

Although the line is drawn relative to the current end point, the angle is measured in absolute degrees, using the East-is-0-degrees convention. Using relative coordinates makes sense when you have many angled lines to draw.

5. To finish the lot boundary, you use a shortcut. Type "c" (short for "close") instead of typing the final coordinates (0,0), as follows:

```
To point: c
```

AutoCAD automatically draws a line from the current end point to the beginning of the first line.

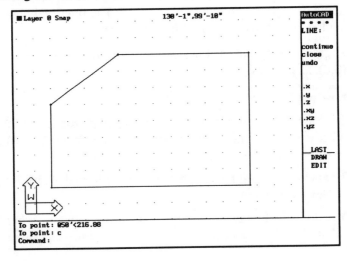

Instead of drafting on paper, you have created your first electronic drawing! More important, you have drawn it full size. That's one of the powerful aspects of CAD. There is no need to use a scale ruler or divide distances by a scaling factor. Everything is drawn full size.

CHANGING LAYERS (Layer)

From the sketch, you know that the lower right corner of the house is located 10' up and 20' in from the lot corner. There are several ways to locate the corner of the house: (1) draw a pair of construction lines 10' and 20' long and erase them later; (2) calculate the coordinates of the corner; (3) draw the house in the corner of the lot and then move the house into position. You'll use the third method to exercise two of AutoCAD's most powerful commands, Pline and Move.

Before you draw the house, you need to change to the layer called "House." Many of AutoCAD's commands, including the Layer command, can be carried out in more than one way (in up to seven different ways, by my count). The flexibility lets you choose the method that suits the way you prefer to work.

The seven ways to invoke a command in AutoCAD methods are:

1. Typing the name at the Command: prompt
2. Picking command names from the side screen menu
3. Using the pop-down menus and dialog boxes
4. Picking an icon from the digitizing tablet overlay menu
5. Programming a button on a multibutton pointing device or auxiliary device
6. Invoking a script, AutoLISP, or ADS (short for AutoCAD Development System) program
7. Abbreviating the command as an alias via the ACAD.PGP file.

In the first hour, you used the Layer Control dialog box to create new layers and set the Lot layer. This time, try typing the word "Layer" at the Command: prompt.

1. To set the House layer, type the Layer command, as follows:
   ```
   Command: layer
   ```

2. The Layer command presents you with 12 options, most of which you ignore for now, as follows:

   `?/Make/Set/New/ON/OFF/Color/Ltype/Freeze/Thaw/LOck/Unlock: s`

For some commands, AutoCAD presents a list of options. To select an option, you need only type its first character. If two (or more) options begin with the same first letter—such as the Ltype and LOck options—you may need to type in the first one or two characters. AutoCAD shows you the minimum number of characters by capitalizing them.

3. Type the letter "s" to invoke the Set option. AutoCAD prompts you to enter the name of the layer, as follows:

   `New current layer <LOT>: house`

Notice that AutoCAD lists the current layer name in angle brackets, <LOT>. This is called the "default" name, which lets you retain the current layer by simply pressing the <Enter> key. To change the working layer to House, type "house" and press <Enter>.

You have set the working layer two different ways: (1) with the Layer Set dialog box; (2) by typing the Layer command name. None is perfect: the first method requires that you make several picks with the pointing device; the other requires several keystrokes.

You probably find you prefer one of the two methods. For myself, I find the dialog box fastest if I need to control more than one layer at a time, while typing in the Layer command is the fastest way to control a single layer.

4. The Layer command repeats its 12-option prompt. Press <Enter> to cancel the command and return to the Command: prompt.

   ```
   ?/Make/Set/New/ON/OFF/Color/Ltype/Freeze/Thaw/LOck/Unlock:
       <Enter>
   Command:
   ```

Look at the status line to confirm that AutoCAD has changed the working layer from "Layer LOT" to "Layer HOUSE."

DRAWING THE HOUSE OUTLINE (Pline, Object Snap)

When you drew the lot boundary with the Line command, you created what looks like a continuous line. In fact, each line segment is an independent entity.

To remedy this, AutoCAD has a special type of line called the "polyline." As the prefix "poly" suggests, a polyline is a line made up of many features—lines, arcs, varying widths—all connected together as a single object. The Pline (short for polyline) command draws polylines in AutoCAD.

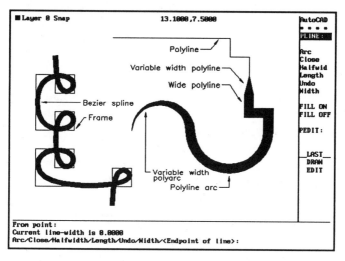

1. Draw the house outline as a polyline, as follows:

   Command: **pline**

2. Like the Line command, the Pline command prompts you for the point from which to begin drawing.

   From point: **int**
   of: **<pick lower right corner of lot>**

3. Instead of specifying a coordinate, you ask AutoCAD to find a geometric feature by using "object snap." When you type "int" (short for intersection) AutoCAD attempts to snap to the nearest intersection, rather than snapping to the nearest 1" you specified with the Snap command in hour one. Since the Int snap overrides the 1" snap, this is sometimes referred to as "object snap override."

AutoCAD has ten geometric object snaps:

Mode	Object Snap	Meaning
cen	CENter	center of arc or circle
end	ENDpoint	end of line or arc
ins	INSertion point	of block or text
int	INTersection	intersection of lines, arcs, circle

25

Mode	Object Snap	Meaning	(Continued)
mid	MIDpoint	middle of line or arc	
nea	NEArest	nearest point	
nod	NODe	point	
per	PERpendicular	perpendicular to line, arc, circle	
qua	QUAdrant	0-,90-,180-,270-degree on circle	
tan	TANgent	tangent to line, arc or, circle	

You use some of the other object snap modes later.

When you type "int," a box appears around the cross hair cursor. The box is called the "object snap aperture" and shows the area in which AutoCAD hunts for the intersection. AutoCAD then curtly prompts you with "of." It is asking you to position the box cursor near the intersection of the two lines. Move the pointing device until the box is over the lower right corner of the lot boundary and press the pick button.

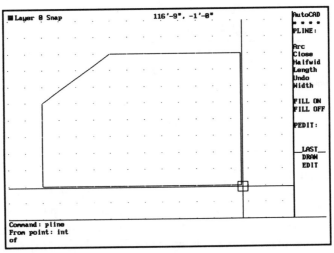

4. AutoCAD then displays one of the longest prompts in its arsenal:

```
Current line-width is 0'-0"
Arc/Close/Halfwidth/Length/Undo/Width/<Endpoint of line>:
    @30'<90
```

The prompt reports that the polyline currently has no width. That doesn't mean the line is invisible. Rather, "zero width" in CAD means that the line is drawn as narrow as possible on the screen and by the printer.

The second line of the prompt displays seven of the Pline command's 22 options. Don't let it intimidate you; for now, you ignore all except the default, Endpoint of line.

5. Draw the remainder of the house outline, as follows:

```
Arc/.../<Endpoint of line>: @3'<0
Arc/.../<Endpoint of line>: @20'<90
Arc/.../<Endpoint of line>: @28'<180
Arc/.../<Endpoint of line>: @50'<270
Arc/.../<Endpoint of line>: c
```

You complete a polyline with the C option, as you did with the Line command.

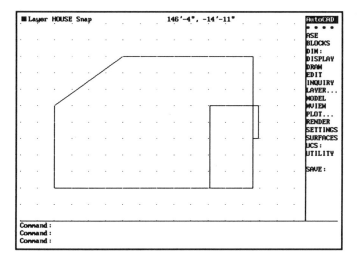

In hour 1, you set the color for the House layer to white; you didn't need to tell AutoCAD to change colors. Because you changed the layer to House, AutoCAD automatically drew the lines in white instead of blue when Lot was the working layer. If you need, you can change colors on the fly with the Color command.

MOVING THE HOUSE INTO POSITION (Move, Redraw)

Now that you've drawn the outline of the house, you move it into position with the Move command.

1. When you start the Move command, AutoCAD asks you what you want to move, as follows:

```
Command: move
Select objects: <pick house>
```

AutoCAD changes the cross hair cursor into a small box cursor, called the "pick cursor." Move the cursor to any part of the polyline making up the outline of the house and press the pick button. The entire house outline is "highlighted." Depending on your graphics board, the highlighting might show as a broken line, a brighter line, or a flashing line. This is AutoCAD's way of letting you know it found the object you picked.

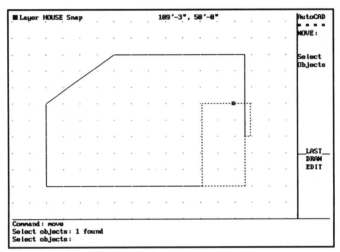

2. AutoCAD lets you select more than one object to move:
   ```
   Select objects: <Enter>
   ```

However, you only need to move the one polyline. Press <Enter> to end the selection process.

3. Like drawing a line, the Move command needs to know a from-point and a to-point. The Move command calls the from-point the "base point," as follows:
   ```
   Base point or displacement: 0,0
   ```

4. Now AutoCAD wants to know where you want to move the selected objects. The Move command calls the to-point the "second point," as follows:
   ```
   Second point or displacement: -20',10'
   ```

The coordinates (-20',10') tell AutoCAD that you want the house moved 20 feet left (X = -20') and ten feet up (Y = 10'). AutoCAD instantly relocates the house. The Move command shows you a powerful aspect of CAD: no eraser dust!

5. The lot boundary probably has a portion missing due to the house moving. You repair the boundary with the Redraw command, as follows:

```
Command: redraw
```

The Redraw command cleans up the screen by redrawing the background and all objects. The screen flashes briefly as AutoCAD completely redraws the drawing.

ADDING THE STREET AND DRIVEWAY
(Fillet, Mirror, Save)

The final drafting you do this hour is of the driveway and the street. Before you begin drawing them, change to the Roads layer.

```
Command: layer
?/Make/Set/New/ON/OFF/Color/Ltype/Freeze/Thaw/LOck/Unlock: s
New current layer <house>: road
```

With the Road layer set, you draw the driveway and street outlines. First you draw the upper roadwork; later you duplicate the lower driveway and street outline with a single command.

1. Use the Line command to draw the upper driveway and street outline, as follows:

```
Command: line
From point: int
of: <pick upper right corner of house>
To point: @28'<0
To point: @40'<90
To point: <Enter>
```

2. If you make a mistake in entering coordinates, such as 40 instead of 40', the line is drawn only 40 inches long. You can "back up" and undraw the incorrect line with the "u" option (short for "undo"), as follows:

```
To point: @40<0
To point: u
To point: @40'<0
```

3. To add the curb return (the arc joining the driveway and street) use AutoCAD's Fillet command. The Fillet command draws an arc between two intersecting lines. The lines don't have to physically meet; AutoCAD takes care of extending the lines so that the arc is drawn between them. Unfortunately, you have to use the Fillet command twice: once to set the radius of the arc; then to create the fillet, as follows:

```
Command: fillet
Polyline/Radius/<Select two objects>: r
Enter fillet radius <0'-0">: 3'
```

4. With the fillet radius set at three feet, repeat the Fillet command to perform the actual filleting, as follows:

```
Command: <Enter>
FILLET Polyline/Radius/<Select two objects>:
    <pick driveway line>
Second object: <pick street line>
```

AutoCAD automatically shortens the two lines to fit the 3-foot arc between them.

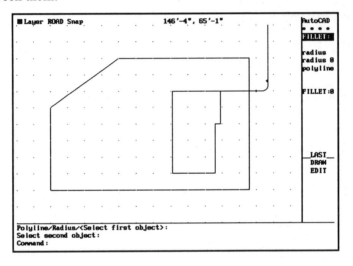

You needed to use the Line command and two applications of the Fillet command to create the upper driveway and street outlines. One of the most important concepts behind computer-aided anything is that you should never have to draw the same line twice. To illustrate the power of this concept, use the Mirror command to duplicate the lower driveway and street line *without having to draw them!* The Mirror command creates a mirrored copy of a set of objects.

5. Start the Mirror command, as follows:

```
Command: mirror
```

6. AutoCAD asks you to select the objects you want to mirror, just as did the Move command, as follows:

```
Select objects: <pick the driveway line>
Select objects: <pick the curb return>
Select objects: <pick the street line>
Select objects: <Enter>
```

7. AutoCAD needs you to specify an imaginary line about which it mirrors the objects you just picked:

```
First point of mirror line: mid
of: <pick center of garage entrance>
Second point: per
of: <pick right-hand lot boundary>
```

The length of the mirror line is not important but the angle is crucial. For this reason you used two new object snap modes: "mid" to find the midpoint of the garage entrance, and "per" to ensure the mirror line is perpendicular to the lot boundary, as shown.

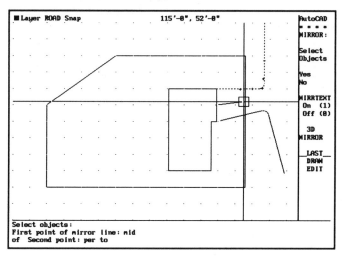

8. At this point, AutoCAD gives you the option of erasing the old objects, the two lines and arc you picked. In most cases, as in this one, you don't want them erased:

```
Delete old objects? <N> n
```

AutoCAD draws the lower driveway and street outline as a perfect mirror image of the upper set, as shown in the following illustration.

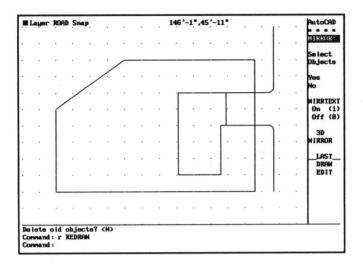

You have now drawn the outline of the lot, house, and roadways. The work you have done is valuable and it is important that you save the drawing to disk.

Use the Save command to store the yard drawing on disk. The dialog box appears on the screen, with the Yard drawing name in the **File:** text box. Press <Enter> to save the drawing.

PUTTING THE DRAWING ON PAPER (Plot)

While it is more efficient (and environmentally aware) to create and store a drawing on a computer, you may want to print a copy of the drawing on paper. That lets you mark up the drawing with notes or show off your progress to your friends!

AutoCAD Release 12 has one command to output the drawing on paper. The Plot command sends the drawing to:

- dot-matrix printers, with brand names such as Epson and IBM ProPrinter
- laser printers, such as Hewlett-Packard's LaserJet
- pen plotters, such as the HP DraftMaster
- electrostatic and thermal plotters
- PostScript laser printers
- raster file formats, such as GIF, PCX, and TIFF.

The following series of dialog boxes assume you have a laser printer compatible with the Hewlett-Packard LaserJet attached to your computer. The commands and prompts for other printers and plotters may differ slightly.

1. You use the Plot command to create a check plot of the Yard drawing, as follows:
   ```
   Command: plot
   ```

The Plot dialog box appears.

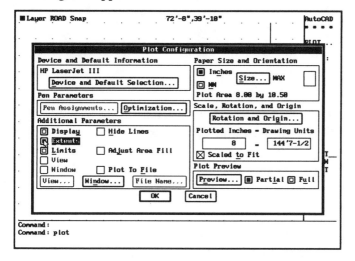

2. The Plot Configuration dialog box has a confusing array of options. For a check plot, you ignore nearly all of them. Click on the box next to Extents (along the left side, under Additional Parameters). The Extents option ensures that everything in your drawing is plotted on the paper.

3. A laser printer normally places the drawing on the paper in portrait mode; however, the drawing better fits a landscape sheet of paper. Click on the **Rotation and Origin...** button, which displays a second dialog box called Plot Rotation and Origin.

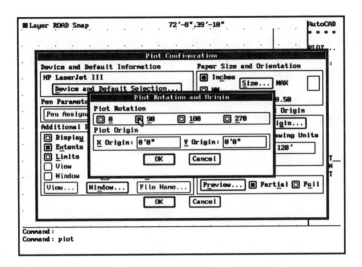

4. Click on the box next to **90** to rotate the drawing by 90 degrees. Click on **OK** to exit the dialog box.

5. To quickly check how the drawing fits the paper, click on the **Preview...** button (in the lower right, under Plot Preview). A second dialog box, called Preview Effective Plotting Area, appears on the screen. The red rectangle shows the plotable area of the paper; the blue rectangle shows the extents of the drawing. Since the two rectangles mostly overlap, you know that the plot will turn out all right. Click on the **OK** button to exit the preview dialog box.

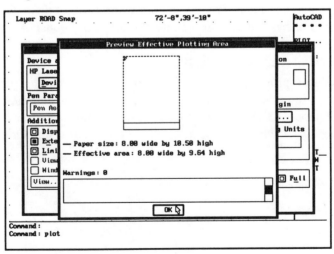

6. When the Plot Configuration dialog box reappears, click on the **OK** button. AutoCAD calculates the area that the drawing takes up on the paper and asks you to check that the printer has paper. When you are ready, press <Enter> to begin the plot.

```
Effective plotting area:  8.00 wide by 9.64 high
Position paper in printer.
Press RETURN to continue or S to Stop for hardware setup:
    <Enter>
```

7. As AutoCAD sends the drawing data to the printer, it reports the number of scanlines it has sent.

```
Regeneration done 100%
3150 raster data scan lines to be sent.
Sending scan line: 16
Scan lines complete.
Plot Complete.
Command:
```

AutoCAD converts its vector drawing into the raster format (called scanlines) required by the LaserJet printer. If you find the plot takes too long, you can reconfigure the LaserJet for a lower resolution, such as 150dpi.

Congratulations! You've drafted your very first drawing using a computer. You can date the drawing and save it as a memento of your introduction to computer-aided drafting.

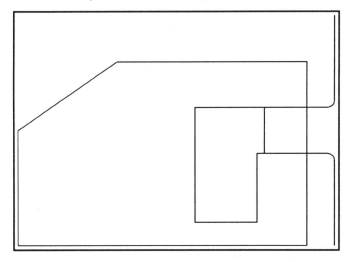

In the next chapter, you learn how AutoCAD makes repetitive drafting a snap. You also learn how to draw arcs and circles and add hatching to the drawing.

HOUR THREE

ADDING DETAILS TO THE LANDSCAPE PLAN

INTRODUCTION

In the last hour, you created the outlines of the lot, the house, and the roadways. This hour, you add details to the yard, such as the lawn, trees, and a pool.

DIVIDING THE LOT (Setvar, Sketch)

The yard has a lawn and a garden area. To draw the boundary between the two areas, you use the Sketch command. The Sketch command records the movements of your pointing device, much like the Etch-A-Sketch drawing toy. The movement is recorded as a series of lines or as a polyline. If you have a digitizing tablet, the Sketch command is good for tracing maps.

1. Before starting the Sketch command, make sure the working layer is set to lawn, as follows:

```
Command: layer
?/Make/.../Unlock: s
New current layer <ROAD>: lawn
?/Make/.../Unlock: <Enter>
```

2. To ensure that AutoCAD records the lawn/garden boundary as a polyline, set the Skpoly (short for sketch as polyline) system variable, as follows:

```
Command: setvar
Variable name of ?: skpoly
New value for SKPOLY <0>: 1
```

The Setvar command lets you change the value of many of AutoCAD's nearly 200 system variables. When Skpoly has a value of 0 (is turned off), the sketch is recorded as a series of lines. By turning Skpoly on, the sketch is recorded as a single polyline.

3. Now you can go into sketch mode by entering the Sketch command, as follows:

```
Command: sketch
Record increment <0'-0">: 5'
```

The "Record increment" is the distance your pointing device moves before AutoCAD records the sketch line. The meaning of this becomes clearer when you begin sketching. Using a fine record increment (say 1") creates a more accurate sketch but takes up a lot of memory. Here, you use a coarse increment of 5' and later smooth out the result.

4. The Sketch command presents a new series of prompts:

```
Sketch.  Pen eXit Quit Record Erase Connect.
```

The first word, Sketch., is a reminder that you are in sketch mode. The other words (including the period at the end) are options of the Sketch command.

5. Move the cursor until you are at the upper edge of the lot boundary at about the midpoint of the diagonal line (you cannot use object snap modes while sketching). When you press the pick button, AutoCAD responds with:

```
<Press pick button>
<Pen down>
```

With the "pen" down, you are now in drawing mode. As you move the pointing device, you see a white rubberband line stretch from the starting point.

6. When you move the pointing device more than five feet, the line changes to red (if your computer has a color monitor) and remains fixed. A new rubberband line appears.

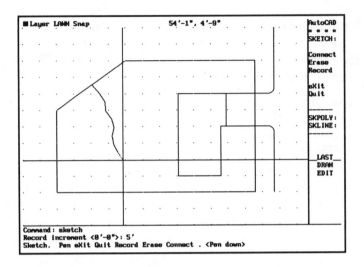

7. Slowly and carefully move your pointing device to the opposite lot line. You may find sketching easier with a digitizing tablet than with a mouse. As you move the pointing device, AutoCAD records your movements as a series of straight, connected, 5'-long lines.

8. When you get to the opposite lot line, press the pick button again. AutoCAD responds:

```
<press pick button>
<Pen up>
```

You are now free to move the pointing device without having AutoCAD record your movements.

9. Now record the sketched polyline, as follows:

```
Sketch.  Pen eXit Quit Record Erase Connect. r
1 polyline with 15 edges recorded.
```

AutoCAD notes that you have drawn one polyline with 15 segments and turns the sketched polyline to green, the color of the layer Lawn.

10. To leave sketch mode, type x for exit, as follows:

```
Sketch.  Pen eXit Quit Record Erase Connect. x
Nothing recorded.
Command:
```

AutoCAD gives the erroneous error message, "Nothing recorded," and returns you to the Command: prompt. You can safely ignore the error message; AutoCAD has, in fact, recorded what you sketched.

SMOOTHING THE SKETCH LINE (Pedit)

Here is the reason you created the sketch as a polyline: you can now use the Pedit (short for polyline edit) command to smooth the straight polyline sketch segments into a flowing curve. If you had used the Sketch command with plain lines, you couldn't smooth them.

1. To edit the sketched polyline, begin the Pedit command, as follows:

```
Command: pedit
Select polyline: <pick sketched line>
```

Pick the sketch polyline.

2. The Pedit command has many options. Its purpose is to let you change the look of a polyline. You use the Spline curve option to smooth the straight lines into a flowing curve, as follows:

```
Close/Join/Width/Edit vertex/Fit/Spline/Decurve/Ltype gen/
    Undo/eXit <X>: s
```

The sketched lines disappear and are replaced by a smooth curve. Technically, AutoCAD has calculated the curve as a cubic Bezier curve based on the sketch frame.

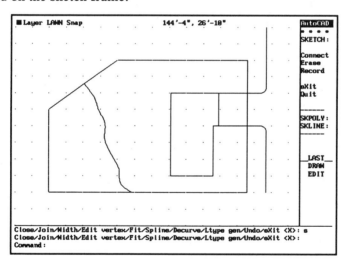

3. To exit the Pedit command, just press <Enter>, as follows:

```
Close/.../eXit <X>: <Enter>
Command:
```

The default is the X option, short for exit.

CLOSING THE SKETCH LINE (Modal Editing)

You have created the boundary between lawn and garden, but how do you tell the difference? One way is to add a grass symbol to the lawn area. In AutoCAD, this is done with the BHatch (short for boundary hatch) command. You apply a hatch pattern to a drawing in two steps: (1) draw a hatch perimeter; (2) apply the hatch pattern inside the perimeter.

AutoCAD Release 12 has commands to automatically create the hatch perimeter and apply the hatch pattern automatically. Your drawing needs the hatch perimeter to contain the pattern. You can use the lawn/garden boundary as part of the hatch perimeter, but you'll need to close the gaps. Otherwise, the pattern might "leak" out and cover the entire drawing.

1. Create a new layer to hold the hatch boundary, as follows:

```
Command: layer
?/Make/.../Unlock: m
New layer name: hatch
?/Make/.../Unlock: <Enter>
```

The Make option creates the new Hatch layer and sets it as the current working layer, all in a single command.

2. Zoom into where the lawn-garden boundary meets the upper lot line, as follows:

```
Command: zoom
All/Center/Dynamic/Extents/Left/Previous/Vmax/Window/
    <Scale(X/XP)>: w
First point: <pick>
Other point: <pick>
```

The Window option of the Zoom command lets you specify the rectangular area on the screen you want magnified. When you pick two "points," you specify the two opposite corners of the rectangle (see following figure).

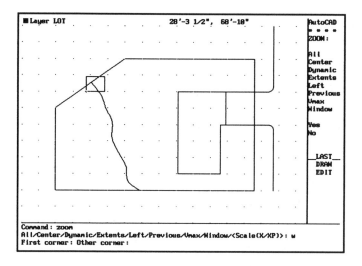

Pick two points on the screen very close to the intersection. AutoCAD changes the view to display the gap between the sketch line and the lot line. If you can't see a gap, use the Zoom Window command again.

3. Start the Pedit command to close the gap.

```
Command: pedit
Select polyline: <pick sketched line>
Close/Join/Width/Edit vertex/Fit/Spline/Decurve/Ltype gen/
    Undo/eXit <X>: e
```

4. Select the Edit vertex option. AutoCAD displays an X-marker at the end of the sketch line and a second set of options:

```
Next/Previous/Break/Insert/Move/Regen/Straighten/Tangent/
    eXit <N>: m
```

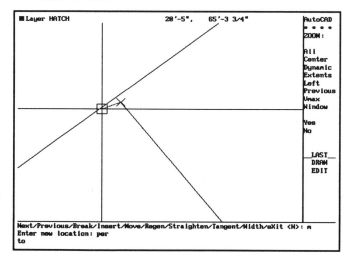

5. Select the Move option. AutoCAD prompts you to:
   ```
   Enter new location: per
   ```

6. To ensure that the gap is precisely closed, use PERpendicular object snap. AutoCAD asks, perpendicular to what?
   ```
   to: <pick lot line>
   ```

AutoCAD extends the end of the sketch line to the lot line, closing the gap.

A FASTER WAY TO CLOSE THE SKETCH LINE
(Non-modal editing)

We repeat the exercise for the other end of the sketch line but by a different method. Earlier, we began the Pedit command, then selected the polyline to edit. This is called "verb-noun" editing or "modal" editing. The verb is the command (Pedit); the noun is the object (the polyline). Modal editing means that you first go into a mode (the Pedit command mode) before performing the action.

New to AutoCAD Release 12, you have the option to first pick the object, then move or stretch it into place. This is called "noun-verb" editing or "non-modal" editing. Non-modal editing is a faster way to edit.

1. Use the Zoom All command to see the full drawing, then use Zoom Window to enlarge the lower end of the sketch line, as follows:
   ```
   Command: zoom
   All/.../Window/<Scale(X/XP)>: a
   Command: zoom
   All/.../Window/<Scale(X/XP)>: w
   First point: <pick>
   Other point: <pick>
   ```

2. In hour one, we pointed out the small box at the center of the cross hair cursor. This is called the "pickbox." When AutoCAD displays the pickbox, you are allowed to pick an object without first starting an editing command. Pick the sketch line. Notice how one or more blue boxes appear on the sketch line, including one at the very end. The blue boxes are called "grips," since they let you grip objects.

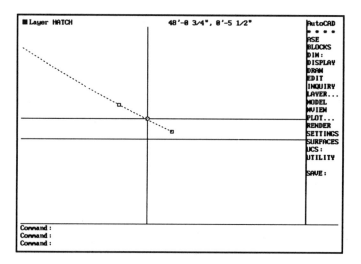

3. Now pick the blue box at the end of the sketch line. It turns solid red; this is known as a "hot" grip since editing commands affect it but not the "cold" blue boxes. In addition, a prompt appears in the command area:

```
** STRETCH **
<Stretch to point>/Base point/Copy/Undo/eXit: per
to <pick lot line>
```

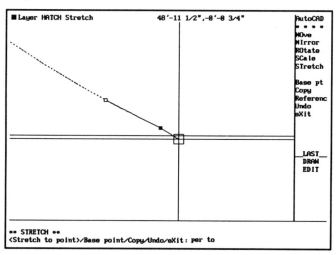

To ensure an exact fit, use the PERpendicular object snap again. AutoCAD moves the sketch line to the lot line.

4. Use the Zoom All command to see the entire drawing again.

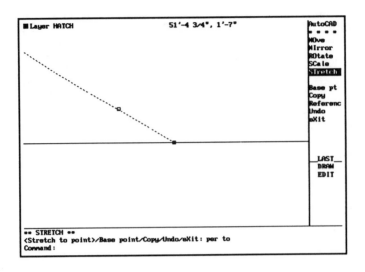

CREATING THE HATCH BOUNDARY (BPoly)

With the gaps closed, create the hatch boundary with the BPoly (short for boundary polyline) command.

1. Start the BPoly command, as follows:

   Command: **bpoly**

AutoCAD displays the Polyline Creation dialog box.

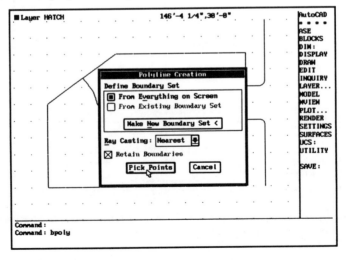

2. The dialog box has several buttons. Click on the **Pick Points** button. The dialog box disappears and AutoCAD prompts:
```
Select internal point <pick>
```

Pick a point anywhere on the lawn area, such as between the sketch line and the house outline.

3. AutoCAD goes through some calculations to find the boundary area:
```
Selecting everything visible...
Analyzing the selected data...
Select internal point <Enter>
```

AutoCAD highlights the boundary it found. Press <Enter> to exit the selection process.

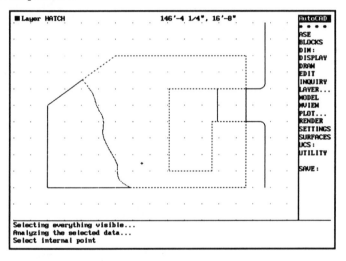

4. AutoCAD draws the boundary polyline on the Hatch layer.

APPLYING THE LAWN HATCHING PATTERN (BHatch)

With the hatch boundary in place, you can now use the BHatch command to apply the grass hatch pattern.

1. First, switch back to the Lawn layer, as follows:
```
Command: layer
?/Make/.../Unlock: s
New current layer <HATCH>: lawn
?/Make/.../Unlock: <Enter>
```

2. Start the BHatch command and AutoCAD displays the Boundary Hatch dialog box:

Command: **bhatch**

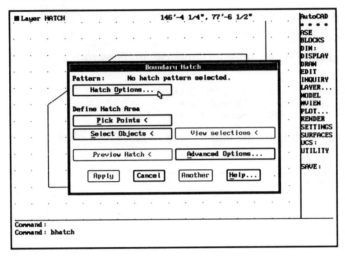

3. The first order of business is to select a hatch pattern. Click on the **Hatch Options...** button. AutoCAD displays a second dialog box, Hatch Options.

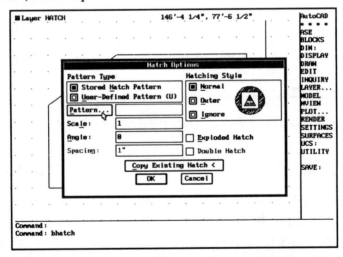

4. Now click on the **Pattern...** button. AutoCAD displays a third dialog box, called Choose Hatch Pattern, which illustrates the hatch pattern samples.

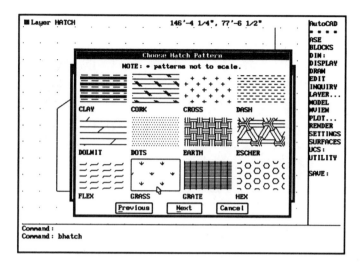

5. Click on the **Next** button until the GRASS hatch pattern appears. Click on the grass pattern; AutoCAD returns to the Hatch Options dialog box.

6. Next, you need to decide the scale factor. Use a large scale factor, such as 50, since hatching (like sketching) can be memory intensive. Enter 50 in the text box next to **Scale:** and click on the **OK** button.

7. AutoCAD returns you to the Boundary Hatch dialog box. To apply the pattern, click on the **Pick Points <** button. The dialog box disappears and AutoCAD prompts:
   ```
   Select internal point <pick>
   ```

Pick the same location you did for creating the boundary polyline. AutoCAD spends a few seconds thinking:
```
Selecting everything visible...
Analyzing the selected data...
Select internal point <Enter>
```

8. AutoCAD highlights the boundary; press <Enter> to end boundary selection.

9. The Boundary Hatch dialog box reappears. Click on the **Apply** button. Note how precisely AutoCAD applied the hatch pattern and how it automatically clips the pattern along boundaries. Try doing a hatch pattern that neatly and that quickly by hand!

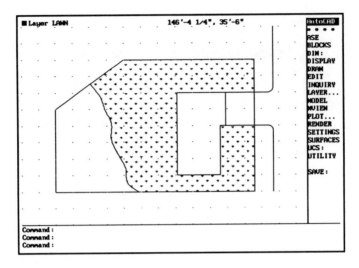

With all this hard work on your drawing, it's a good idea to save the drawing to the computer's hard disk with the Save command... right now!

CREATING A TREE SYMBOL (Circle, Array)

Let's add some trees and shrubs to the garden area. You can draw the symbol for a tree out of a circle and an array of lines. After you draw one tree symbol, you add several more with a single command.

1. Before starting the first tree, make sure the working layer is set to Plants, as follows:

```
Command: layer
?/Make/.../Unlock: s
New current layer <LAWN>: Plants
?/Make/.../Unlock: <Enter>
```

2. Use the Circle command to draw a six-inch-radius circle, as follows:

```
Command: circle
3P/2P/TTR/<Center point>: <pick in garden area>
Diameter/<Radius>: 6
```

AutoCAD has five different ways to draw a circle. Here you have used the most common method: pick the circle's center point and specify the radius of the circle. By specifying a radius of 6, AutoCAD draws a circle with a one-foot diameter.

3. The one-foot circle looks very small on the screen. The Zoom command lets you see your work more clearly.

```
Command: zoom
All/Center/Dynamic/Extents/Left/Previous/Vmax/ Window/
    <Scale(X/XP)>: w
First point: <pick point>
Other point: <pick point>
```

Pick the points on diagonal corners either side of the circle.

4. Now that the tree circle looks larger, it is easier to work with. To draw the array of lines (representing the branches), you draw one line and then use the Array command to create the array.

```
Command: line
From point: cen
of <pick circle>
To point: <pick point>
To point: <Enter>
```

Here you used the CENter object snap to begin the line at the precise center of the circle. The other end of the line can go just beyond the edge of the circle

5. Repeat the branch line 24 times with the Array command, as follows:

```
Command: array
Select objects: L
1 found Select objects:  <Enter>
Rectangular or Polar array (R/P) <R>: p
Center point of array: cen
of <pick circle>
Number of items: 25
Angle to fill (+=ccw, -=cw) <360>: <Enter>
Rotate objects as they are copied? <Y> <Enter>
```

AutoCAD quickly draws 24 more lines around the circle, completing the tree symbol.

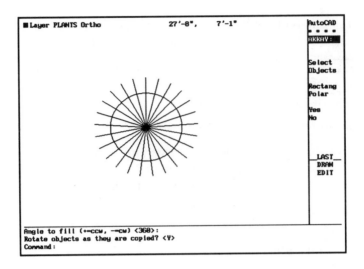

When the Array command asks you to select the objects to array, you can respond with the letter "L" (short for Last). This is AutoCAD's shorthand notation for selecting the last object drawn *still visible on the screen.* "L" works as a response whenever a command prompts you with "Select objects:."

You typed in "p" for polar array; the Array command can also create a rectangular array of objects. The Array command has a quirk: if you want to array an object 24 times, you have to specify 25 as the number of items. AutoCAD considers the original item as the first arrayed item.

You can simply press <Enter> for the last two questions. Pressing <Enter> is AutoCAD's shorthand to accept the default value shown in the angle brackets, such as <360> degrees.

MAKING A SYMBOL (Block)

Although CAD lets you draw a symbol, such as the tree symbol, fairly quickly, there are many keystrokes involved. You can reduce the keystrokes by turning the symbol into a "block" and then inserting the block into the drawing. Here you add several more trees to the garden area.

1. To turn the tree symbol into a block, use the Block command as follows:

   ```
   Command: block
   ```

2. The Block command asks for the name of the block, here "Tree."

   ```
   Block name (or ?): tree
   ```

You can give the block any name you like up to 31 characters long; for practical purposes, you should keep the name under nine characters.

3. The "insertion base point" is used later by the Insert command as the point where the block is inserted into the drawing. The center of the tree symbol is a logical insertion point; using the CENter object snap ensures a precise pick.

   ```
   Insertion base point: cen
   of <pick circle>
   ```

4. AutoCAD lets you select objects several different ways. So far, you have picked them (one at a time) with your pointing device or with the "L" option. Just as you windowed the zoomed-in view, you can also window the objects you want to select with the "w" option (short for window).

   ```
   Select objects: w
   First corner: <pick corner>
   Other corner: <pick corner>
   26 found Select objects: <Enter>
   ```

You pick the two corners of a rectangle that encompasses the circle and 25 lines making up the tree symbol. Make sure that all 26 objects are inside the selection rectangle, otherwise AutoCAD won't include them.

5. The tree symbol disappears! But don't worry: AutoCAD has stored the block definition in the drawing. It erased the original drawing because it is not a block. To bring back the tree symbol, use the Oops command, as follows:

   ```
   Command: oops
   ```

The tree reappears. The Oops command also returns objects that you accidently erased.

ADDING MANY MORE TREES (Zoom Dynamic, Insert)

Now that the tree symbol is a block, you can insert it into the drawing.

1. First, zoom back out so that you can see more of the garden area, as follows:

```
Command: zoom
All/.../Window/<Scale(X/XP)>: d
```

When you select the Zoom command's Dynamic option, the graphics screen changes to display the Zoom Dynamic screen. Here you see an overview of the entire drawing, with the most recent view outlined with a dashed line (lower right, in the following figure).

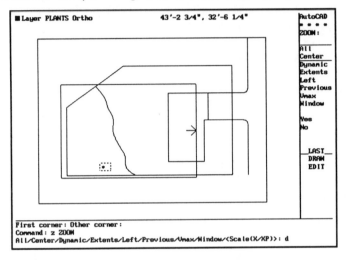

2. When you move your pointing device, the view box moves; this is called "panning."

3. Pressing the pick button changes the "X" in the view box to an arrow. When you move your pointing device, the view box becomes larger or smaller; this is called "zooming."

4. It can be a bit tricky at first, but after some practice you can enlarge the view box and place it around the garden area. Then press <Enter> and AutoCAD displays the new view.

(If you find Zoom Dynamic too frustrating, press <Ctrl>-C instead, do a Zoom All followed by a Zoom Window, as follows:

```
Command: zoom
All/.../ Window/<Scale(X/XP)>: a
Regenerating drawing.
Command: <Enter>
All/.../ Window/<Scale(X/XP)>: w
First corner: <pick>
Other corner: <pick>
```

5. Now insert a 5'-tree with the Insert command, as follows:
   ```
   Command: insert
   ```

6. Supply the Insert command with the name of the block, Tree, and pick a point in the garden area, as follows:
   ```
   Block name (or ?): tree
   Insertion point: <pick a point in the garden area>
   ```

7. When you supply an X-scale factor, AutoCAD draws the block larger or smaller than the original symbol.
   ```
   X scale factor <1> / Corner / XYZ: 5
   ```

By specifying an X-scale factor of 5, AutoCAD draws the block five times larger. Since you drew the original symbol one foot in diameter, the newly inserted tree is five feet in diameter. You can see that it makes sense to draw a symbol to unit size (to the nearest inch or foot): that makes it easy to scale the block during insertion.

8. If you want to stretch or squeeze the block, the Insert command allows you to specify a different Y-scale factor. This is useful for inserting rectangles (such as different sized lumber) based on a unit square.
   ```
   Y scale factor (default=X): <Enter>
   ```

9. You can insert blocks at an angle by responding to the "Rotation angle" prompt with an angle. Since the tree symbol is round, it makes no sense to insert it at an angle.
   ```
   Rotation angle <0.0000>: <Enter>
   ```

10. Add several more trees around the garden area using the Insert command and different X-scale factor (see figure below).

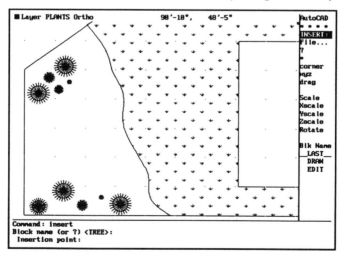

11. Anytime you need to remind yourself of the block names in a drawing, you can use the Insert command as follows:

```
Command: insert
Block name (or ?): ?
Block(s) to list <*>: <Enter>
```

12. AutoCAD flips to the text screen and displays the list of block names that currently exist in the drawing.

```
Defined blocks
      TREE
User           Unnamed
Blocks         Blocks
    1              1
Command: <F1>
```

Here you see there is one block you created, the Defined Blocks, and User Blocks. There is one Unnamed Block, which is the grass hatch pattern. AutoCAD stores hatch patterns (and associative dimensions) as blocks in the drawing. Press <F1> to return to the drawing screen.

DRAWING THE POND (Ellipse, Offset)

Drawing the garden pond illustrates another pair of AutoCAD commands. You can draw the oval-shaped pond with the Ellipse command and add the pond's edging with the Offset command.

1. Switch to the Pond layer:

```
Command: layer
?/Make/.../Unlock: s
New current layer <PLANTS>: pond
?/Make/.../Unlock: <Enter>
```

2. The pond is an oval 15 feet long and 5 feet wide. Draw the pond with the Ellipse command as follows:

```
Command: ellipse
```

3. AutoCAD has four different ways to draw an ellipse. Here you draw the ellipse by specifying the major and minor axes. You can pick the starting point of the ellipse anywhere in the garden area.

```
<Axis endpoint 1>/Center: <pick>
```

4. The other end of the pond is 15 feet away, with the pond angling at 300 degrees.

```
Axis endpoint 2: @15'<300
```

5. And the pond is five feet wide:

```
<Other axis distance>/Rotation: 5'
```

6. You could draw the rock edging of the pond by reusing the Ellipse command but it probably wouldn't be precisely centered. Instead, the Offset command creates a concentric ellipse, as follows:

```
Command: offset
Offset distance or Through <Through>: 1'
Select object to offset: <pick ellipse>
Side to offset? <pick outside ellipse>
Select object to offset: <Enter>
```

The Offset command also creates parallel lines, parallel polylines, and concentric circles and arcs.

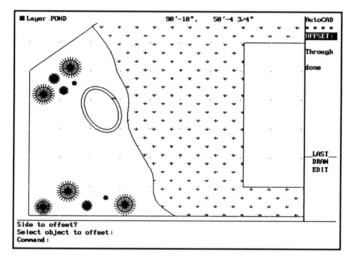

Remember to save your work with the Save command. To see the progress you are making in learning AutoCAD, you can plot your drawing with the Plot command.

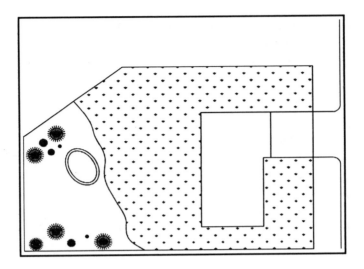

In this hour, you added details to the landscape plan. With drawing commands such as Sketch, BPoly, BHatch, Circle, and Ellipse you drafted the lawn, trees, and pond. Editing commands such as Pedit, Array, Insert, and Offset made the tedious job of drawing details much faster.

Next hour, you learn some of AutoCAD's inquiry commands to get information out of the drawing. You also add a fence, change colors of objects, and modify the shape of the pond.

HOUR FOUR

CHANGING THE LANDSCAPE

INTRODUCTION

In the last hour, you added details to the drawing, such as the lawn, some trees, and a pond. This hour you learn how to change parts of the yard and how to get information out of the drawing.

CHANGING THE LOOK OF LINES
(Linetype, Change, Ltscale)

When you drew the lot lines in the first hour, they showed up on the screen as a solid line. However, lot lines are usually shown in a dashed pattern. Just as AutoCAD comes with several hatching patterns, it also includes a number of line patterns, called "linetypes."

To change from a solid line (called "continuous" by AutoCAD) to a dashed linetype takes two steps: (1) load the linetype; (2) change the line to the new linetype. If necessary, start AutoCAD and open the Yard drawing.

1. First, do a Zoom All so that you see the entire drawing on the screen, as follows:
   ```
   Command: zoom
   All/.../<Scale (X/XP)>: a
   Regenerating drawing.
   ```

2. The linetype definitions are stored in a separate definition file (called ACAD.LIN) on the hard drive. Before you can use a linetype, you have to load it into the drawing, as follows:

```
Command: linetype
?/Create/Load/Set: L
```

The Linetype command lets you list the linetypes currently in the drawing with the "?" option. At this point, only the Continuous linetype is loaded. The Create option lets you create a new linetype on the fly, while the Set option sets the working linetype, much like the Layer command's Set option.

3. The Load option loads the linetype definitions from the file ACAD.LIN:

```
Linetype(s) to load: *
```

When you type "*" (shorthand for load *all* linetype definitions), AutoCAD pops up a dialog box. Pick the **OK** button.

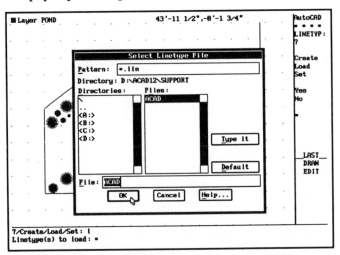

4. AutoCAD then lists the linetype names as it loads them:

```
Linetype BORDER loaded.
Linetype BORDER2 loaded.
Linetype BORDERX2 loaded.
Linetype CENTER loaded.
Linetype CENTER2 loaded.
Linetype CENTERX2 loaded.
Linetype DASHDOT loaded.
Linetype DASHDOT2 loaded.
Linetype DASHDOTX2 loaded.
Linetype DASHED loaded.
Linetype DASHED2 loaded.
Linetype DASHEDX2 loaded.
```

```
Linetype DIVIDE loaded.
Linetype DIVIDE2 loaded.
Linetype DIVIDEX2 loaded.
Linetype DOT loaded.
Linetype DOT2 loaded.
Linetype DOTX2 loaded.
Linetype HIDDEN loaded.
Linetype HIDDEN2 loaded.
Linetype HIDDENX2 loaded.
Linetype PHANTOM loaded.
Linetype PHANTOM2 loaded.
Linetype PHANTOMX2 loaded.

?/Create/Load/Set: <Enter>
```

I find it easier to load all linetypes at once, rather than loading the one or two that you currently need. That saves you from going through the load procedure each time you need another linetype.

5. The Change command changes a number of attributes of an object, including changing linetypes. You use it here to change the lot lines from continuous to border. Since the hatch boundary obscures the lot lines, freeze the layer Hatch, as follows:

```
Command: layer
?/Make/Set/New/ON/OFF/Color/Ltype/Freeze/Thaw/LOck/Unlock: f
Freeze layer name <POND>: hatch
?/Make/Set/New/ON/OFF/Color/Ltype/Freeze/Thaw/LOck/Unlock:
    <Enter>
```

Freezing a layer makes AutoCAD completely ignore any information on that layer.

6. Start the Change command and pick the five lines that make up the lot's boundary, as follows:

```
Command: change
Select objects: <pick>
1 selected, 1 found Select objects: <pick>
1 selected, 1 found Select objects: <pick>
1 selected, 1 found Select objects: <pick>
1 selected, 1 found Select objects: <pick>
1 selected, 1 found Select objects: <Enter>
```

7. At this point, you can change the shape of the entity or change its properties. Later you get to change an entity's shape; right now you want to change the linetype. Select the "p" (short for properties) option and the "lt" (short for linetype) option, as follows:

```
Properties/<Change point>: p
Change what property (Color/Elev/LAyer/LType/Thickness)? lt
```

8. When prompted, type the name of the linetype that the lot lines should take on: Border.

```
New linetype <BYLAYER>: border
```

9. Press <Enter> to exit the Change command.

```
Change what property (Color/Enter/LAyer/LType/Thickness)?
<Enter>
```

10. You see the lot lines redraw on the screen *very s-l-o-w-l-y* and yet look solid. That's because the dash-dot pattern is being drawn at a very small scale. You enlarge the linetype scale with the Ltscale command, as follows:

```
Command: ltscale
```

11. Type the same scale factor as you used for the hatch pattern, 50, as follows:

```
New scale factor <1.0000>: 50
Regenerating drawing.
```

AutoCAD now redraws the lot lines with the border linetype visible. That process was a lot easier than using an eraser shield!

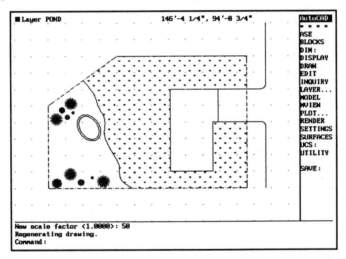

CHANGING LINE LENGTHS

As an example of how the Change command changes the size of an entity, extend the edge of the street to the bottom of the screen, as follows:

1. Before starting the Change command, press function key <F8> to turn on ortho mode. This ensures the changes are made perfectly vertical. Type the Change command and pick the bottom road line, as follows:

```
Command: <F8> <Ortho on> change
Select objects: <pick bottom road line>
1 selected, 1 found Select objects: <Enter>
```

2. When prompted with <Change point>, pick a point at the bottom of the screen below the end of the road line. It doesn't matter if you are directly below the line.

```
Properties/<Change point>: <pick point>
```

AutoCAD extends the line to the bottom of the screen.

3. Turn off ortho mode by pressing <F8> again.

```
Command: <F8> <Ortho off>
```

CHANGING THE LOOK OF THE POND (Stretch)

So far, you have used several editing commands to change objects. You've used Pedit to modify polylines, non-modal editing to stretch the sketch line, and the Change command to alter the appearance of lines.

One of AutoCAD's most powerful editing commands is called Stretch. The Stretch command lets you take part of an object and stretch it wider or thinner. Here you apply it to the pond to change its shape.

1. First, zoom in on the pond so that you see it more clearly, using the Zoom Window command as follows:

```
Command: zoom
All/.../<Scale (X/XP)>: w
First corner: <pick>
Other corner: <pick>
```

2. Start the Stretch command, as follows:

```
Command: stretch
Select objects to stretch by window...
```

3. Despite the Stretch command's prompt to the contrary (it says "stretch by window"), crossing mode is the *only* object selection mode you can use the first time you select objects with the Stretch command, as follows:

```
Select objects: c
```

"C" is short for "crossing," an object selection mode similar to the window mode you used with the Zoom command. In this case, AutoCAD selects all objects within the selection rectangle *and all objects crossing or touching the rectangle* (see following figure). You may find crossing mode somewhat faster than Window mode since you don't have to draw as large a rectangle.

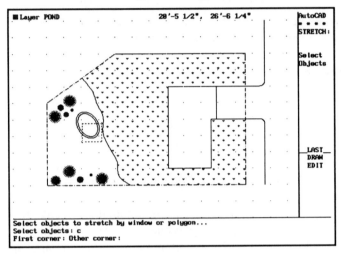

AutoCAD has 17 options that you can use during object selection, as shown in the following table. I find that I use only a few of the options, such as <pick>, W, C, L, P and <Enter>.

Mode	Abbreviation	Meaning
Object	<pick>	select a single object
Window	W	select all objects within a rectangular window
Window Polygon	WP	select all objects within a polygonal window
Crossing	C	select object crossing and within a rectangular window
Crossing Polygon	CP	select all objects crossing and within a polygon
Fence	F	select objects along a fence polyline
Box	B	W or C mode, depends on cursor movement
Automatic	AU	<pick>, W, or C mode, depending on pick point
Single	SI	select first object encountered
Last	L	select most recently drawn object

Mode	Abbreviation	Meaning	(Continued)
Previous	P	select most recently selected object	
Multiple	M	delay database scanning	
Undo	U	remove most recent selection group	
Remove	R	enter remove-objects mode	
Add	A	enter add-objects mode	
End	<Enter>	end object selection	
Cancel	<Ctrl>-C	cancel object selection	

4. Pick two corners of a rectangle that covers part of the pond, as follows:

```
First corner: <pick>
Other corner: <pick>
2 found Select objects: <Enter>
```

Notice how the crossing box is a dashed rectangle, which differs from the solid rectangle used with the window box. If the pond were entirely inside the object selection rectangle, the Stretch command would only move the pond, not stretch it.

5. To tell AutoCAD how much you want the pond stretched, pick two points that indicate the distance:

```
Base point: <pick near pond>
New point: <pick away from pond>
```

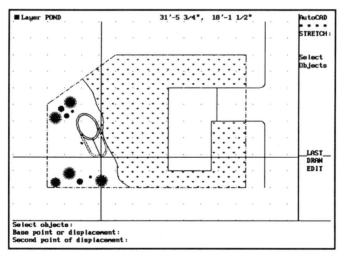

6. You have now created a whole new look to your pond! If you don't like it, you can undo the stretch with the U command, as follows:

```
Command: u
U: STRETCH
... and try stretching the pond again.
```

7. If the pond isn't exactly where you want it, you relocate it with the Move command. Move the pond closer to the lawn, as follows:

```
Command: m
```

Here you used another of AutoCAD's shortcuts. "M" is the abbreviation for the Move command. The complete list of command name abbreviations (called aliases) are:

Alias	Command
A	Arc
C	Copy
CI	Circle
DV	Dview
E	Erase
L	Line
LA	Layer
M	Move
MS	Mspace
P	Pan
PS	Pspace
PL	Pline
R	Redraw
Z	Zoom

8. Continue the Move command, as follows:

```
MOVE Select objects: c
First corner: <pick>
Other corner: <pick>
1 found Select objects: <Enter>
Base point or displacement: <pick edge of pond>
Second point of displacement: <pick new location>
```

MEASURING THE AREA OF THE LAWN (Area)

You've seen how to create a drawing in AutoCAD and how to change the drawing. AutoCAD is able to return to you in a useful form some of the information stored in the drawing.

A common piece of information is the area of objects. If you need to know how much fertilizer to buy for your lawn, you use the Area command to find the lawn's area.

1. Zoom out to the full view if you haven't already done so:

```
Command: zoom
All/Center/Dynamic/Extents/Left/Previous/Vmax/Window/<Scale
    (X/XP)>: a
Regenerating drawing.
```

2. Thaw and set the Hatch layer to reuse the hatch outline:

```
Command: layer
?/Make/Set/New/ON/OFF/Color/Ltype/Freeze/Thaw/LOck/Unlock: t
Thaw layer name: hatch
?/Make/Set/New/ON/OFF/Color/Ltype/Freeze/Thaw/LOck/Unlock: s
New current layer <POND>: hatch
?/Make/Set/New/ON/OFF/Color/Ltype/Freeze/Thaw/LOck/Unlock:
    <Enter>
```

Thawing a layer turns off the freezing action you performed earlier.

3. Start the Area command, as follows:

```
Command: area
```

The Area command adds and subtracts areas. Its entity option finds the area of shapes, such as circles and polygons.

```
<First point>/Entity/Add/Subtract: e
```

4. Pick the hatch outline:

```
Select circle or polyline: <pick hatch boundary>
Area = 628486.6 square in. (4364.490 square ft.),
Perimeter = 380'-8 1/2"
```

Your answer varies depending on where you located the garden/lawn boundary. Now you know: you need fertilizer for about 4,700 square feet of lawn.

ADDING A FENCE (Point Filters, List, Dist)

You've decided to add a fence to the backyard. You can use AutoCAD to help you plan the materials you'll need. After you draw the fence as a polyline, you find out from AutoCAD how long that line is. Later, you let AutoCAD automatically add equispaced fence posts.

1. First, switch the working layer to House, as follows:

```
Command: layer
?/Make/Set/New/ON/OFF/Color/Ltype/Freeze/Thaw/LOck/Unlock: s
New current layer <HATCH>: house
?/Make/Set/New/ON/OFF/Color/Ltype/Freeze/Thaw/LOck/Unlock:
    <Enter>
```

2. If you turned the INTersection object snap off, turn it back on:

```
Command: osnap
Object snap modes: int
```

3. The fence is drawn as a 4"-wide polyline. Along the way, you'll use a number of object snap modes and point filters. Begin the Pline command, as follows:

```
Command: pline
```

4. Start the polyline at the middle of the upper house line. Use the MIDdle object snap override to precisely locate the polyline's starting point, as follows:

```
From point: mid
of <pick upper house line>
Current line-width is 0'-0"
```

5. To change the width of the polyline from zero to four inches, use the "w" option, as follows:

```
Arc/Close/Halfwidth/Length/Undo/Width/<Endpoint of line>: w
Starting width <0'-0">: 4"
Ending width <0'-4">: <Enter>
```

(You can specify a different starting and ending width to produce tapered polylines.)

6. Now that the starting point and width are set, continue drawing the fence. Follow the path shown by the arrowheads in the following figure.

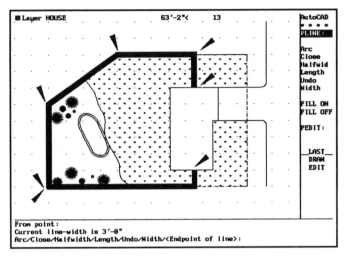

```
From point:
Current line-width is 3'-0"
Arc/Close/Halfwidth/Length/Undo/Width/<Endpoint of line>:
```

```
Arc/.../<Endpoint of line>: per
to <pick upper lot line>
Arc/.../<Endpoint of line>: <pick upper right of diagonal>
Arc/.../<Endpoint of line>: <pick lower left of diagonal>
Arc/.../<Endpoint of line>: <pick lower left corner of lot>
```

Pause the picking action here.

7. When you get to the bottom of the house, you get into a bit of tricky geometry. You want the fence to end at the same relative location as its starting point. Fortunately, AutoCAD finds that point for you through the use of "point filters."

Use the .y point filter on the bottom line of the lot, as follows:

```
Arc/.../<Endpoint of line>: .y
of <pick lower left corner of lot line>
```

Point filters let you enter a coordinate with a combination of screen pointing and keyboarding. When you use the ".y" point filter, you are telling AutoCAD that you want to pick the y-coordinate on the screen and will supply the x-coordinate from the keyboard. AutoCAD has six point filters, as shown in the following table:

Filter	Picks	AutoCAD Needs
.x	x	y- and z-coordinates
.y	y	x- and z-coordinates
.z	z	z- and y-coordinates
.xy	x and y	z-coordinate
.xz	x and z	y-coordinate
.yz	y and z	x-coordinate

As you can probably tell from the presence of the z-coordinate table, point filters are also used in three-dimensional drafting.

8. You're not sure of the x-coordinate, which is located somewhere along the bottom line of the lot. AutoCAD reminds you with the "(need X)" prompt, as follows:

```
(need X): mid
of <pick upper house line>
```

Pick the middle of the upper house line with the MIDdle object snap override.

9. Complete the fence by drawing the last polyline segment PERpendicular to the lower house line, as follows:

```
Arc/.../<Endpoint of line>: per
to <pick lower house line>
Arc/.../<Endpoint of line>: <Enter>
```

10. Now that you've drawn the fence, use the List command to tell you the length, as follows:

```
Command: list
Select object: <pick fence polyline>
1 selected 1 found
Select objects: <Enter>
```

AutoCAD flips to the text screen and lists line after line of information:

```
            POLYLINE  Layer: HOUSE
                      Space: Model space
               Color: 7 (white)    Linetype: CONTINUOUS
        Open
starting width      0'-4"
  ending width      0'-4"

            VERTEX    Layer: HOUSE
                      Space: Model space
               Color: 7 (white)    Linetype: CONTINUOUS
         at point, X=    85'-0"  Y=    60'-0"  Z=    0'-0"
starting width      0'-4"
  ending width      0'-4"

...et cetera

          END SEQUENCE  Layer: HOUSE
                      Space: Model space
            Color: 7 (white)    Linetype: CONTINUOUS
        area   893948.3 sq in (6207.975 sq ft)
        length 260'-0"
```

The List command is giving you every piece of information about the polyline that AutoCAD has stored in its database. Most of the information is about the vertices (the corners). The total length of the polyline is shown at the end of the listing: 260 feet. You now know how much fencing you need.

Press <F1> to flip back to the graphics screen.

11. You can also measure distances directly on the drawing. The Dist command (short for distance) measures the distance between two points. Find the shortest distance from the house to the pond, as follows:

```
Command: dist
First point: nea
to <pick inside edge of pond>
Second point: per
to <pick house wall>
Distance = 33'-11 1/2",  Angle in X-Y Plane = 0.0000,
Angle from X-Y Plane = 0.0000
Delta X = 33'-11 1/2",  Delta Y = 0'-0",  Delta Z = 0'-0"
```

The beeline distance from house to pond is nearly 34 feet. The value on your drawing may differ, depending on where you located the pond.

INSTALLING FENCE POSTS (Measure, Divide)

The names of AutoCAD commands tend to describe their function. The Line command draws lines, the Plot command plots the drawing and the Change command changes objects. The Measure command, however, doesn't measure distances. Instead, it marks a line or polyline, as does its first cousin, the Divide command. The easiest way to understand Measure and Divide is by going through an example. Add fence posts to the fence with the Measure command. For the from point, pick a point in any clear area of the drawing.

1. First, you need to create a fence post. The fence post is simply a 1' square drawn as a polyline, as follows

```
Command: pline
From point: <pick>
Current line-width is 0'-4"
Arc/.../<Endpoint of line>: w
Starting width <0'-4">: 1'
Ending width <1'-0">: <Enter>
Arc/.../<Endpoint of line>: @1'<0
Arc/.../<Endpoint of line>: <Enter>
```

2. Now turn the square post symbol into a block, as follows:

```
Command: block
Block name (or ?): post
Insertion base point: mid
of <pick square>
```

```
Select objects: <pick square>
Select objects: <Enter>
```

The post disappears as AutoCAD turns it into a block. By selecting the insertion point as the middle of the post, you ensure that the post is precisely centered along the fence.

3. Now that the fence post is a block, you have AutoCAD apply a fence post every five feet with the Measure command, as follows:

```
Command: measure
Select object to measure: <pick fence polyline>
<Segment length>/Block: b
Block name to insert: post
```

4. You want the post block to align with the diagonal portion of the fence line.

```
Align block with object? <Y> y
Segment length: 5'
```

AutoCAD (nearly instantly) draws in 52 fence posts along the fence line.

The Divide command is very similar, except that you specify the number of posts to place along the fence, rather than the distance between posts.

5. Curiously, AutoCAD leaves out the first fence post. You have to add the missing post with the Block command, as follows:

```
Command: insert
Block name (or ?): post
Insertion point: int
of <pick fence/house intersection>
X scale factor <1> / Corner / XYZ: <Enter>
Y scale factor (default=X): <Enter>
Rotation angle <0.0000>: <Enter>
```

That adds the fifty-third fence post. If the length of the fence polyline in your drawing differs, then AutoCAD may not have drawn the last fence post either. Use the Move command to move the nearest post to the end.

Remember to save the work you have done on the drawing. You may also want to plot out the drawing.

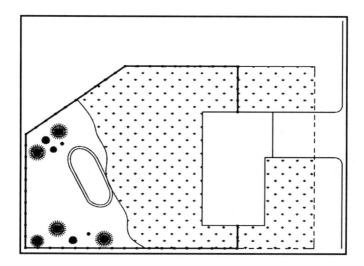

In this hour, you learned more about modifying the drawing with the Change and Stretch commands. You also learned about linetypes and how to calculate areas. Next hour, you learn how to add text, dimensions, and a title block to the drawing.

HOUR FIVE

ADDING NOTES AND DIMENSIONS

INTRODUCTION

In the last hour, you changed parts of the yard and learned how to get some information out of the drawing. This hour, you add the finishing touches by drawing callouts on the drawing, dimensioning the yard, and inserting a predrawn border around the drawing. You also learn how to save and restore named views of the drawing.

Bring the yard drawing into AutoCAD and do a Zoom All to make the full drawing visible. Make sure that the working layer is Text.

ADDING A NOTE TO THE DRAWING (Text)

With the yard plan largely complete, you now add callouts to describe the different parts of the yard.

1. In AutoCAD, you add callouts with the Text command, as follows:
   ```
   Command: text
   ```

2. Pick a starting point for the note within the house outline.
   ```
   Justify/Style/<Start point>: <pick>
   ```

3. The height of the text should be large enough to be legible when you plot the drawing. If you have been plotting the drawing on an A-size sheet of paper, you can make an estimate of the drawing scale with the following calculation:

```
Height of drawing in real units: about 120'
Width of A-size paper: about 8"
Therefore, scale factor: about 120'*12/8" = 1:180
```

Now that you know the drawing scale, you determine how large to make the text with the following calculation:

```
Height of plotted text: about 3/16"
Height of text in real units: 3/16" * 180 = 34"
```

To get 3/16"-high text in the plotted output, you need to enter text 34" high on the AutoCAD drawing, as follows:

```
Height <0'-3 1/2">: 34"
```

If you have been plotting the drawing on larger paper, such as B- size, the text should be half as large, or 17".

4. Press <Enter> for the rotation angle since you want horizontal text, as follows:

```
Rotation angle <0.0000>: <Enter>
```

5. Type the label "House" and press <Enter>; AutoCAD immediately draws the word House.

```
Text: House
```

6. Zoom in on the word "House" to get a closer look at it, as follows:

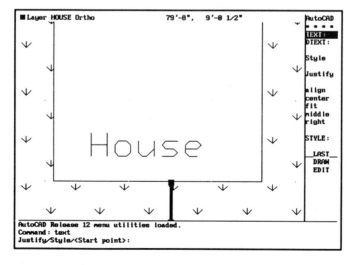

```
Command: zoom
All/.../<Scale(X/XP)>: w
First corner: <pick>
Other corner: <pick>
```

The text looks kinda ugly, like it was created by a computer! This is the basic font, called TXT, that is in every new AutoCAD drawing. Fortunately, AutoCAD comes with a large number of text fonts that look better than this one.

CHANGING THE TEXT FONT (Style)

Just like you have to load hatch patterns and linetypes into an AutoCAD drawing file, you have to load additional text fonts. This is done with the Style command. It's easiest to use the pop-down menus to load a text font.

1. Move the cursor to the status line and pick **[Draw]** from the menu bar.
2. From the pop-down menu, pick **[Text >]**.
3. From the second pop-down menu, pick **[Set Style...]**.

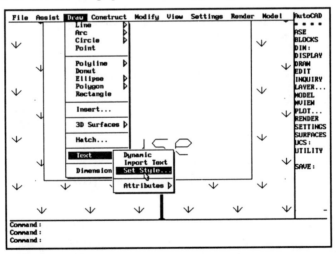

4. An icon menu appears on the screen. This menu displays 20 of AutoCAD Release 12's 38 fonts. As you see, some fonts are suitable for international projects; others are symbols.
5. Picking the **Next** button displays several fonts converted from PostScript Type 1 PFB files. The Compile command converts

any other PFB font files you may have into AutoCAD's SHX font format.

6. Pick the **Previous** button to return to the first icon menu. Click on the **Roman Simplex** font. This is a clear and smooth-looking font that resembles the drafter's ISO text. Click **OK**.

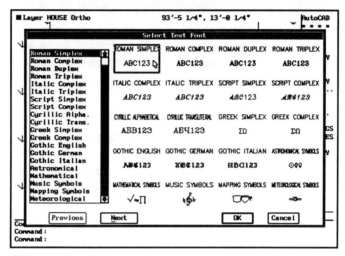

7. In the command prompt area, the Style command asks you a number of questions. These let you make subtle (and not so subtle) changes to the text font, which creates a text style. You can create many styles from a single font.

First, AutoCAD automatically gives the style the same name as the font, RomanS (short for Roman Simplex), as follows:

```
Text style name (or?): romans
New style
Font file <romans>: romans
```

8. Leave the style height at 0" by pressing <Enter>, as follows:
```
Height <0'-0">: <Enter>
```

A style height of 0" has a special meaning in AutoCAD. It means that you specify the height of the text later with the Text command. If you specify a height with the Style command, the height is fixed; you can no longer change it during the Text command.

9. Make the text a little bit narrower by specifying a width factor of 0.85, as follows:
```
Width factor <1.00>: .85
```

The narrower width allows you to fit 15% more text into the same space, yet leaves the text perfectly legible.

10. Give an obliquing angle of five degrees, as follows:
    ```
    Obliquing angle <0.0000>: 5
    ```

A slight forward slant of five degrees makes the text look a little nicer when plotted.

11. For the remaining questions answer <Enter> since you don't want the text to print backwards, upside-down, or vertically:
    ```
    Backwards? <N> <Enter>
    Upside-down? <N> <Enter>
    Vertical? <N> <Enter>
    ROMANS is now the current text style.
    ```

You may have expected the word House to change to the new RomanS font. No such luck. That would have happened with the very early versions of AutoCAD, since old AutoCAD could only handle one font in a drawing at a time. Nowadays, AutoCAD maintains as many styles as you care to define into the drawing.

Instead, all text from now on is drawn with the RomanS font. To see this, add the callout "Pool" to the pond. Later, you correct the mislabeled callout.

12. First, save the current view with the View command. This makes it easier for you to later return to the same zoomed-in view.
    ```
    Command: view
    ?/Delete/Restore/Save/Window: s
    View name to save: house
    ```

13. Now zoom out with the Zoom All command, then zoom into the pool with the Zoom Window command, as follows:
    ```
    Command: zoom
    All/.../<Scale(X/XP)>: a
    Regenerating drawing.
    Command: <Enter>
    ZOOM All/.../<Scale(X/XP)>: w
    First point: <pick>
    Other point: <pick>
    ```

14. Now that you see the pond area more clearly, use the Text command, as follows:
    ```
    Command: text
    ```

15. This time, use one of AutoCAD's 15 justification modes, as follows:

```
Justify/Style/<Start point>: j
Align/Fit/Center/Middle/Right/TL/TC/TR/ML/MC/MR/BL/BC/BR: a
First text line point: <pick one end of the pond>
Second text line point: <pick other end of pond>
```

Here you selected the Align justification, which draws text fitted between two points. All of AutoCAD's text justification modes are listed in the following table:

Justification	Meaning
Start point	baseline left
Align	fitted between two points
Fit	fitted with constant text height
Center	baseline center
Middle	exact center of text
Right	baseline right
TL	top left
TC	top center
TR	top right
ML	middle left
MC	middle center
MR	middle right
BL	bottom left
BC	bottom center
BR	bottom right

I find that I mostly use only five of the modes: left, right, middle, center, and align.

16. Since the Align option's pick points define the width and angle of the text, AutoCAD doesn't ask for the height or rotation angle. Instead, the Text command goes straight to the prompt:

```
Text: Pool
```

The word "Pool" is drawn with the RomanS text style.

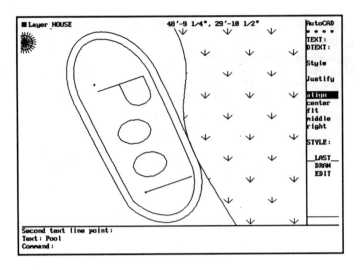

CHANGING EXISTING TEXT
(Ddmodify, Ddedit, Rotate)

1. The word Pool is in the correct text style, but House isn't. To change the style of the word House, you use the Ddmodify command. First, return to the previously saved view, as follows:
   ```
   Command: view
   ?/Delete/Restore/Save/Window: r
   View name to restore: house
   ```

2. Start the Ddmodify command and select the word House, as follows:
   ```
   Command: ddmodify
   Select objects to modify: <pick House text>
   ```

3. After picking the word House, AutoCAD displays the Modify Text dialog box.

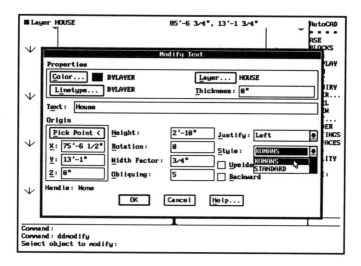

The dialog box displays everything about text that you could change in AutoCAD. For the word House, the dialog box indicates (from top to bottom):

- color: bylayer
- layer: house
- linetype: bylayer
- thickness: 0"
- text: House
- x,y,z-coordinates of insertion point: 75'-6 1/2", 13'- 1", 0
- text height: 2'-10"
- rotation angle: 0 degrees
- width factor: 3/4"
- obliquing angle: 5 degrees
- justification: left
- style: Standard
- upside down: no
- backward: no
- handle name: none

Only the entity handle name (its hexadecimal code number in the drawing database) cannot be changed. "Bylayer" means the text takes on the color and linetype defined by the layer.

4. Move the cursor to the down arrow next to **Style: STANDARD** and click the pointing device's pick button.

5. A list box drops down, listing the two text styles currently loaded into the drawing. Click on **ROMANS,** then click on the **OK** button.

6. The dialog box disappears and AutoCAD redraws the word House in the RomanS font.

7. Oops! "Pool" should read "Pond." If you need to change the wording of text, you use the Ddedit command, as follows:

```
Command: zoom
All/.../<Scale(X/XP)>: a
Command: ddedit
<Select a TEXT or ATTDEF object>/Undo: <pick Pool word>
```

The Edit Text dialog box pops up on the screen.

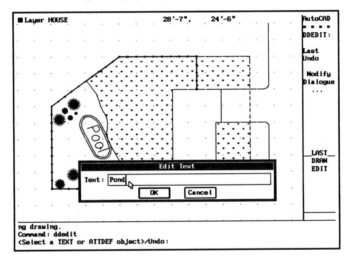

8. Pick beside the word Pool in the dialog box, backspace over "ol" and type **nd.**

9. Pick the **OK** box at the bottom of the dialog box. AutoCAD instantly replaced Pool with Pond.

10. Exit the Ddedit command by pressing <Enter> again:

```
<Select a TEXT or ATTDEF object>/Undo: <Enter>
```

11. Now add the street name, as follows:

```
Command: text
Justify/Style/<Start point>: <pick point on street>
Height <2'-10">: <Enter>
Rotation angle <0.0000>: 90
Text: Donlyn Avenue
```

By specifying a rotation angle of 90 degrees, AutoCAD draws the text sideways.

12. If you picked the wrong rotation angle, you can rotate the text after the fact. Pick the text, as follows:
    ```
    Command: <pick text>
    ```

13. A blue box appears at the text's insertion point. Click on the blue box again so that it turns solid red. Select the Base point option, as follows:
    ```
    ** STRETCH **
    <Stretch to point>/Base point/Copy/Undo/eXit: b
    Base point: <pick red square again>
    ```

14. Specify the ROtate option and an angle of 180 degrees, as follows:
    ```
    ** ROTATE **
    <Rotation angle>/Base point/Copy/Reference/eXit: 180
    ```

AutoCAD draws the text flipped over. As an alternative, you can use the pointing device to show AutoCAD how you want the object rotated (as shown in the following illustration). The ROtate option changes the angle of any object in the drawing.

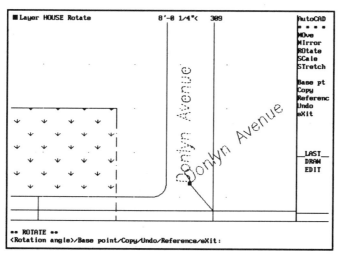

A FASTER WAY TO DEAL WITH TEXT (Dtext)

Just as the Ddedit command is a more efficient method to change text than the Change command, the Text command has a more efficient associate called Dtext (short for dynamic text). The Dtext command lets you place text all over the drawing without needing to reinvoke the Text command each time and repeatedly answering the same prompts.

1. Use the Dtext command to add more callouts to the drawing, as follows:

```
Command: dtext
Justify/Style/<Start point>: <pick near bottom of drawing>
Height <2'-10">: <Enter>
Rotation angle <90.0000>: 0
Text: 34486 Donlyn Avene
```

The first part of the Dtext prompts are exactly the same as for the Text command. Notice, however, the little box cursor is displayed and each letter is drawn as you type it. This is different from the Text command which draws the entire sentence after you complete it. Misspell "Avene" as shown; we correct it later.

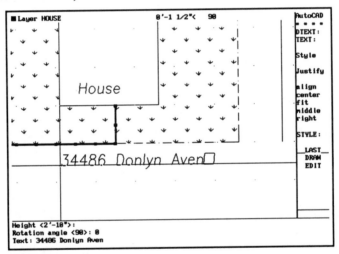

2. When you press <Enter> at the end of Avene, the Text: prompt reappears. Notice the spelling mistake in Avene; you backspace with the Backspace key <BS> and type the correction, as follows:

```
Text: <BS><BS>ue
```

3. Type the next line, as follows:

```
Text: Abbotsford BC
```

You don't need to start the Dtext command again, as you would with the Text command. Dtext automatically jumps to the next line below.

4. Now move the cursor to near a clump of trees and press the pick button. Dtext is ready for you to type more words:

```
Text: Birch trees
Text: <move cursor to other trees> Western
Text: Red Cedar
Text: <Enter>
```

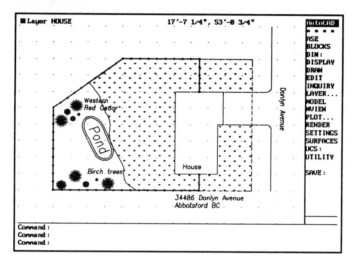

5. Press <Enter> to end the Dtext command. When you do, AutoCAD rewrites all the text as left justified.

At this point, it is a good idea to save your work using the Save command.

REDUCING TEXT DISPLAY TIME (Qtext, Regen)

A lot of text in a drawing slows down the display speed. AutoCAD has a special command, called Qtext (short for Quick Text), that changes text into rectangular outlines.

1. Change the text into outlines with the Qtext command, as follows:

```
Command: qtext
ON/OFF <Off>: on
```

2. The call-outs look no different! AutoCAD doesn't change the text until the next regeneration. Force a screen regeneration with the Regen command, as follows:

```
Command: regen
Regenerating drawing.
```

The callouts have changed to a series of rectangular outlines.

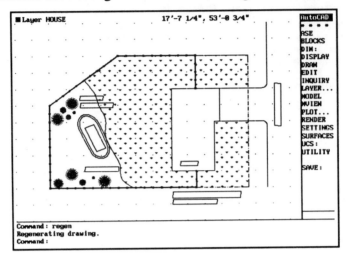

3. Change the outlines back to note, as follows:

```
Command: qtext
ON/OFF <On>: off
Command: regen
Regenerating drawing.
```

DIMENSIONING THE YARD (Dimscale, Dim)

With several callouts placed on the drawing, you may want to add dimensions to the lot. This is done with the Dim (short for dimensioning) command, one of the most involved commands of AutoCAD's repertoire. Fortunately, AutoCAD comes preconfigured with most dimensioning variables set to reasonable values. Most of the time, you only need to set one variable, the scale of the dimensions.

1. First, set the dimensioning scale with the Dimscale command. The dimension scale ensures that the arrowheads and text are drawn a size appropriate for the drawing. Start the Dimscale command, as follows:

```
Command: dimscale
```

2. For a dimension scale of 1.0, AutoCAD draws the dimensioning text 0.18" high, which is close to 3/16". However, as you saw with the Text command, the text needs to be large enough to be legible when plotted. To find the new value of Dimscale, divide the plotted text height by the default text height, as follows:

```
Plotted text height      34"
------------------- = - ----- = 188.89
Default text height      0.18"
```

Thus, the value of the dimension scale should be about 190, as follows:

```
New value for DIMSCALE <1.0000>: 190
```

3. Since all of the lot dimensioning takes place at intersections, turn on INTersection object snap mode, as follows:

```
Command: osnap
Object snap modes: int
```

4. Now go into dimensioning mode with the Dim command, as follows:

```
Command: dim
Dim:
```

AutoCAD changes the prompt from Command: to Dim: to remind you that you are in dimensioning mode. No AutoCAD commands work while the Dim: prompt appears, except those relating to dimensioning and transparent commands.

HORIZONTAL AND CONTINUOUS DIMENSIONS (Hor, Con)

1. Dimension the lower lot line, as follows:

```
Dim: hor
First extension line origin or RETURN to select: <pick A>
Second extension line origin: <pick B>
Dimension line location (Text/Angle): <pick below the lot
line>
Dimension text <116'>: <Enter>
```

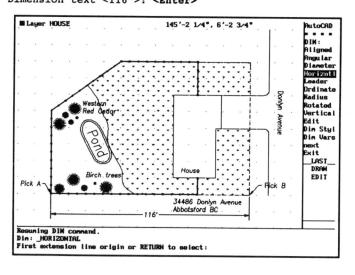

Press <Enter> at the Dimension text prompt; AutoCAD knows the length of the line and reports it in the angle brackets. If you like, you can type in any other dimension or text. AutoCAD automatically draws all the components of the dimension.

2. Try another horizontal dimension, this time along the top of the lot line:

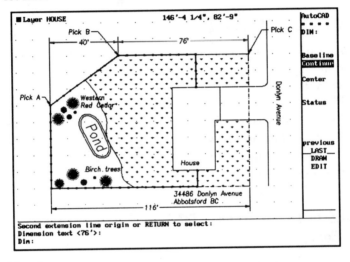

```
Dim: hor
First extension line origin or RETURN to select: <pick A>
Second extension line origin: <pick B>
Dimension line location: <pick>
Dimension text <40'>: <Enter>
```

Notice how AutoCAD draws the extension lines long enough to reach to your pick points.

3. Continue the horizontal dimension with the Con (short for continue) command, as follows:

```
Dim: con
Second extension line origin or RETURN to select: <pick C>
Dimension text (Text/Angle) <76'>: <Enter>
```

Since AutoCAD knows where your last extension line was, it only needs to know the location of the next extension line to draw in the second dimension.

VERTICAL AND BASELINE DIMENSIONS (Ver, Bas)

1. To draw a vertical dimension, you use the Ver command, as follows:

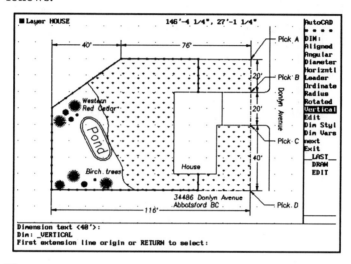

```
Dim: ver
First extension line origin or RETURN to select: <pick A>
Second extension line origin: <pick B>
Dimension line location (Text/Angle): <pick>
Dimension text <20'>: <Enter>
```

2. Use the Con command to continue the vertical dimensions along the right side of the lot at points C and D.

3. A variation on the Con command is the Bas command (short for baseline). Rather than continue a dimension from the previous extension line, Bas dimensions from the original extension line.

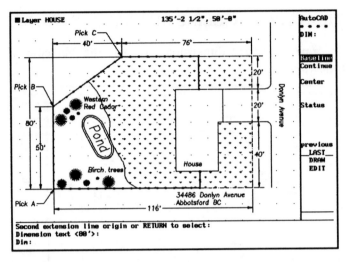

```
Dim: ver
First extension line origin or RETURN to select: <pick A>
Second extension line origin: <pick B>
Dimension line location: <pick>
Dimension text (Text/Angle) <50'>: <Enter>
```

4. Try the Bas command as follows:

```
Dim: bas
Second extension line origin or RETURN to select: <pick C>
Dimension text (Text/Angle) <80'>: <Enter>
```

The Bas and Con commands work with horizontal, vertical, and angled dimensions.

ALIGNED AND RADIAL DIMENSIONS (Ali, Rad)

1. So far, you have dimensioned the angled portion of the lot line with horizontal and vertical dimension commands. To dimension an angled line, you use the Ali command (short for aligned), as follows:

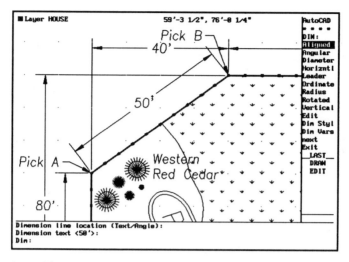

```
Dim: ali
First extension line origin or RETURN to select: <pick A>
Second extension line origin: <pick B>
Dimension line location: <pick>
Dimension text (Text/Angle) <50'>: <Enter>
```

2. The dimensioning commands you have been using present pretty much the same prompts to you. Now try some dimension commands that are a bit different. For example, the Rad command (short for radius) dimensions an arc or circle that you pick, as follows:

```
Dim: rad
Select arc or circle: <pick a driveway radius>
Dimension text (Text/Angle) <3'>: <Enter>
Enter leader length for text: <pick a suitable point>
```

The Rad command gives you some flexibility as to where you want to place the dimension text. As you move the cursor, AutoCAD ghosts in the leader and text.

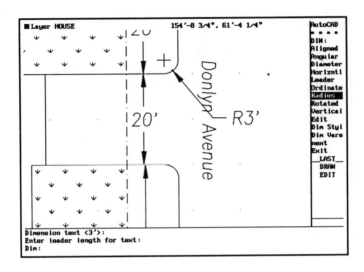

ADDING THE BORDER AND TITLE BLOCK

As a final touch, you add a predrawn border and title block around the drawing. AutoCAD Release 12 includes a drawing called ADESK_ B.DWG, which is a drawing of a border and title block.

The border drawing is inserted with the Insert command. Previously, you inserted Tree and Post blocks that were defined in your drawing. AutoCAD allows you to also insert *any other drawing* into your drawing as a block! This is a great time saver since it means you can use portions of other drawings in your drawing without having to redraw everything.

Inserting another drawing works very similarly to inserting a block into the drawing.

1. First, exit the Dim: prompt and zoom out to give some breathing room around the drawing, as follows:

```
Dim: exit
Command: zoom
All/.../<Scale(X/XP)>: .6
Regenerating drawing.
```

The value of ".6" displays the drawing 60% smaller, in effect zooming out. If you use a number larger than one (such as 2), AutoCAD zooms in, making the drawing appear larger.

2. The Adesk_B.Dwg is stored as a unit-size block. If you insert it into the drawing without applying a scale factor, it appears in the corner as a tiny 1"x1" blob. There are two ways to tell AutoCAD how large to draw the block. One is to calculate the scale factor, as you did with the Tree blocks. The other method is to point on the screen how large you want it; that's what you do here.

Start the Insert command, as follows:

```
Command: insert
Block name (or ?): adesk_b
```

AutoCAD first searches the drawing for a block called "Adesk_B" and then searches the hard disk. It lets you know if it cannot find the block or drawing. (If the file is not on your computer's hard disk, AutoCAD displays the AutoCAD Alert dialog box, with the message, "Can't open file." Don't worry: click on OK and skip to step 7.)

3. Pick an insertion point in the lower left corner of the screen, well away from the drawing, as follows:
```
Insertion point: -40',-60'
```

4. At the following prompt, enter the same scale factor you used for Dimscale:
```
X scale factor <1> / Corner / XYZ: 190
Y scale factor <default = X): <Enter>
```

5. Press <Enter> at the following prompt, since you don't want the border drawn at an angle:
```
Rotation angle <0.0000>: <Enter>
```

AutoCAD draws the border in place (see the plotted figure below).

6. If you want, you can zoom into the title block and add your name and the date with the Dtext command. Remember to save your drawing and plot out the final version (see following figure).

7. Quit AutoCAD after saving in preparation for the next activity.

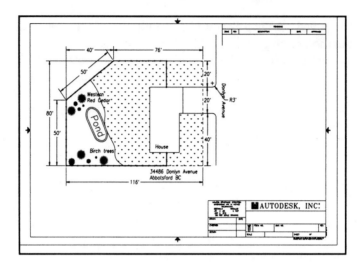

In this hour, you learned how to add callouts to the drawing, dimension the yard, and insert a border around the drawing. This concludes the lessons on drawing in two dimensions. Next hour, you learn how to draw with AutoCAD's three-dimensional drawing tools.

PART II
THREE-DIMENSIONAL DESIGN

HOUR SIX

STARTING A 3D DRAWING

INTRODUCTION

In the first five hours of this book, you learned many of AutoCAD's commands to draw, edit, and plot the landscape plan in two dimensions. AutoCAD also has commands to help you create three-dimensional objects.

Designing in three dimensions is more difficult than in two dimensions because your tools are still 2D. Your computer's display screen, pointing device, and printer all operate on flat surfaces. In this hour, you learn about AutoCAD's aids to 3D designing in a 2D environment using the Advanced Modelling Extension.

Note: If you did not purchase the AME module, you will not be able to follow along in AutoCAD. Read through this material, then load the completed Table.Dwg at the beginning of Hour 8, Viewing in Three Dimensions.

BEFORE YOU BEGIN

To learn about 3D drafting, you can use another example commonly found in your home: the coffee table. The example used for the three-dimensional portion of this book is based on creating and displaying a computer-generated model of a coffee table.

Follow along with the example shown. Or, if you prefer, you can measure the coffee table in your living or family room and create the three-dimensional model on your own.

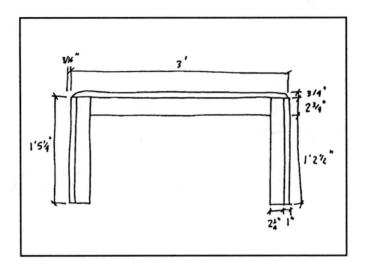

PREPARING FOR DRAWING THE TABLE
(New, Mvsetup, Ddrmodes)

Prepare a new drawing for the coffee table, as follows:

1. Start AutoCAD.

2. Use the New command to begin a new drawing called "Table."
   Command: **new**

In the text box next to New Drawing Name..., type **table**, then click on the **OK** button.

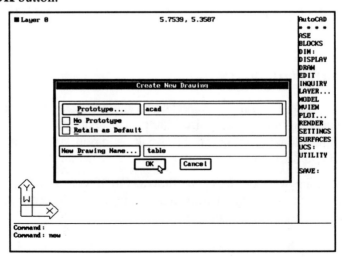

3. Use the Mvsetup (short for make view setup) command to create the four standard engineering views. Mvsetup quickly splits the screen into four viewports (or windows) to show three-dimensional objects from four view points: top, front, side, and isometric.

```
Command: mvsetup
Initializing... MVSETUP loaded.
Paperspace/Modelspace is disabled. The pre-R11 setup will
be invoked unless it is enabled.
Enable Paper/Modelspace? <Y>: y
```

AutoCAD works in two different spaces: (1) model space; and (2) paper space. In the first five hours of this book, you worked (perhaps unknowingly) in model space. There you drew the yard as a full-size computer model. Paper space lets you position the model onto a piece of paper as an aid to producing the plot.

4. The Mvsetup command has several options, of which we use only one. Enter "C" to create the viewports, as follows:

```
Entering Paper space. Use MVIEW to insert Model space
viewports.
Regenerating drawing.
MVSetup, Version 1.15, (c) 1990-1992 by Autodesk, Inc.
Align/Create/Scale viewports/Options/Title block/Undo: c
```

5. Press <Enter> to go ahead with creating viewports, as follows:

```
Delete objects/Undo/<Create viewports>: <Enter>
```

6. AutoCAD switches to the text screen and displays four different styles of viewports Mvsetup can create:

```
Available Mview viewport layout options:
0: None
1: Single
2: Std. Engineering
3: Array of Viewports
Redisplay/<Number of entry to load>: 2
```

Select option 2, which creates the standard engineering arrangement of a drawing.

7. Next, Mvsetup asks for the area of the viewports. Specify the dimensions of an A-size sheet of paper, as follows:

```
Bounding area for viewports. First point: 0,0
Other point: 11,8.5
Distance between viewports in X. <0.0>: <Enter>
Distance between viewports in Y. <0.0>: <Enter>
```

We don't need any space between the viewports, so press <Enter> to keep the spacing at zero inches.

8. Exit the Mvsetup command by pressing <Enter>, as follows:

```
Align/Create/Scale viewports/Options/Title block/Undo:
    <Enter>
```

9. Switch back to model space with the Mspace command, as follows:

```
Command: mspace
```

Look at the four viewports created: there are three different UCS icons showing. In the upper left viewport, the UCS icon is as you are used to seeing it. In the upper right viewport, the UCS icon is slanted; it shows the viewport is an isometric view. The two lower viewports have a broken pencil icon; this means that you cannot draw in these viewports unless you change the user-defined coordinate system first. Why? Some commands work properly only when the x,y-plane is facing you (or when the UCS icon is clearly visible).

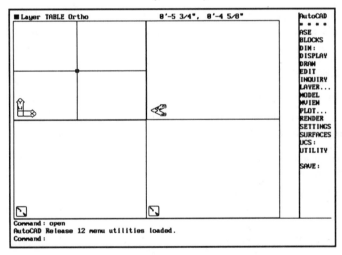

10. Use the Ddunits command to set architectural units to the nearest 1/16th inch.

11. In the first hour, you set the snap, grid, and ortho modes with commands typed from the keyboard. Here is another way to set the modes. Move the cursor to the status line and pick **Settings**.

12. From the pop-down menu, pick **Drawing Aids....**

13. The Drawing Tools dialog box pops up on the screen. Turn the **Ortho** toggle on, turn on **Snap**, set the snap spacing to 1/16", turn on the **Grid** and set the grid spacing to 2". If necessary, use the

<Tab> key to move between fields. Click on the **OK** button to exit the dialog box.

```
■ Layer TABLE Ortho              0'-11 3/8", 0'-6 1/16"        AutoCAD
                                                               ■ ● ● ●
                                                               ASE
                                                               BLOCKS
                                                               DIM:
                                                               DISPLAY
                  ┌─────────── Drawing Aids ───────────┐       T
                  │                                     │       UIRY
     Modes          Snap              Grid                      ER...
     ☒ Ortho        ☒ On              ☒ On                      EL
                                                               EM
     ☒ Solid Fill   X Spacing 1/16"   X Spacing 2"             T...
                                                               DER
                    Y Spacing 0'0-1/16" Y Spacing 0'2"         TINGS
     ☐ Quick Text                                              FACES
                    Snap Angle 0                               :
     ☒ Blips        X Base   0'0"      Isometric Snap/Grid     LITY
                                       ☐ On
     ☒ Highlight    Y Base   0'0"      ◉ Left ☐ Top ☐ Right    E:

              [  OK  ]   [Cancel]   [Help...]


Command: open
AutoCAD Release 12 menu utilities loaded.
Command: '_ddrmodes
```

14. Use the Layer command to make the layer "table" with the color yellow.

15. The coffee table is square in shape. To take advantage of its double symmetry, place the origin (0,0) in the center of the drawing. You do this with the Limits command, as follows:

```
Command: limits
Reset Model space limits:
ON/OFF/<Lower left corner> <0'-0",0'-0">: -20,-20
Upper right corner <1'-0",0'-9">: 20,20
Command: zoom
All/.../<Scale(X/XP)>: a
Regenerating drawing.
```

This sets the limits to (-20,20) and (20,20) and places the origin in the center of the screen. You can see this for yourself by moving the cursor to the center of the screen and watching how the coordinate display gets close to (0'-0",0'-0").

At this point, you have prepared the drawing for designing in three dimensions. It is a good idea to save the drawing with the Save command before continuing on.

LOADING AME INTO AUTOCAD (AME)

AutoCAD has three different ways to draw three-dimensional objects: (1) draw objects at different elevations and give them thickness; (2) draw with 3D lines and planes; (3) use the solids modelling, the easiest method.

Creating a solid model with AutoCAD is similar to architects building massing models. You put together basic shapes—such as boxes, spheres, cylinders, and cones—to create complex shapes. In this hour, you use only boxes in different proportions to create the coffee table.

Note: Every copy of AutoCAD Release 12 includes two versions of the solids modelling feature. If you didn't pay extra for the Advanced Modelling Extension, then you have "Regions," a stripped down version of AME that only works in two dimensions. Check the AutoCAD box: if there is an AME authorization number, you have the full version of AME. If not, you will not be able to follow along with Hours 6 and 7 of this book; pick up again in Hour 8, Viewing in Three Dimensions, by loading the completed TABLE.DWG file from the bonus diskette.

1. Load AME into the AutoCAD drawing environment as follows: Move the cursor to the status line and pick **Model**. When the menu pops down, pick **Utility**, then pick **Load Modeller**.

2. AutoCAD responds, as follows:
   ```
   No modeler is loaded yet. Both AME and Region Modeler are
      available.
   Autoload Region/<AME>: ame<Enter>
   ```

3. An alternative method to steps #1 and #2 is to manually load AME, as follows:
   ```
   Command: (xload "ame")
   ```

Depending on the speed of your computer, AME can take up to a minute to load.

CONSTRUCTING A TABLE LEG (Solbox, Pan)

With the drawing environment set up and AME loaded, you can begin drawing in three dimensions. Start with a table leg. It is made of two pieces of wood butted together, which you can model with two rectangular boxes.

1. Move the cursor to the upper left viewport and press the pick button. The cursor changes from an arrow to the cross hair shape. When the cursor is a cross hair, you are in the working viewport, also called the current viewport. Press **<F7>** to turn on the grid.

2. Use the Solbox command (short for solids box) to draw the first piece of wood, as follows:
   ```
   Command: solbox
   Initializing Advanced Modelling Extension.
   ```

3. Begin drawing the box in the center of the drawing, as follows:
   ```
   Baseplane/Center/<Corner of box>: <0,0,0> <Enter>
   ```

The default coordinates in angle brackets specify the x,y,z-coordinate values of 0,0,0.

4. The first piece of wood has dimensions of 3-1/4"L x 1"W x 17-1/4"H. Use the Length option to specify the three dimensions of the box, as follows:
   ```
   Cube/Length/<Other corner>: L
   Length: 3.25
   Width: 1
   Height: 17.25
   ```

The length is in the x-direction, the width is in the y-direction, and the height is in the z-direction. AutoCAD now takes several seconds to add this data to its solids model database, with the following report:
```
Phase I - Boundary evaluation begins.
1 of 6 of Phase I in process.
Phase II - Tessellation computation begins.
1 of 6 of Phase II in process.
Updating the Advanced Modeling Extension database.
```

Finally, the box is drawn.

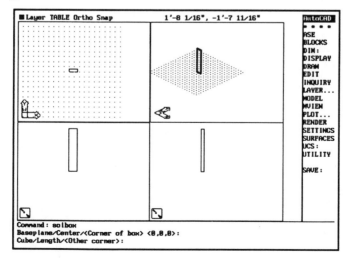

5. The second piece of wood for the table leg has the dimensions of 1"L x 2-1/4"W x 17-1/4"H. It is drawn as a second box adjacent to the first box, as follows:

```
Command: solbox
Baseplane/Center/<Corner of box>: <0,0,0> <Enter>
Cube/Length/<Other corner>: L
Length: 1
Width: -2.25
Height: 17.25
Phase I - Boundary evaluation begins.
1 of 6 of Phase I in process.
Phase II - Tessellation computation begins.
1 of 6 of Phase II in process.
Updating the Advanced Modeling Extension database.
```

AME draws the second part of the table leg.

CHANGING THE VIEWS (Zoom 2, Pan)

If you cannot see all of the legs in all viewports, use the Zoom and Pan commands to move the image about.

1. First use the Zoom command to resize each viewport. Pick a viewport, then use the Zoom command, as follows:

```
Command: zoom
All/.../<Scale(X/XP)>: 2
```

Repeat for each viewport.

2. If you want to center the table leg in a viewport, use the Pan command to move the image over. First, turn off ortho by pressing function key <F8>. Then pick the viewport. Use the Pan command, as follows:

```
Command: <F8> <pick viewport> pan
Displacement: <pick where the leg is now>
Second point: <pick where you want the leg>
Command: <F8>
```

Finally, turn ortho mode back on. Due to a limitation of AutoCAD, you cannot pick the viewport after starting the Pan or Zoom commands. With the views resized and centered, the computer's screen might look something like the following illustration.

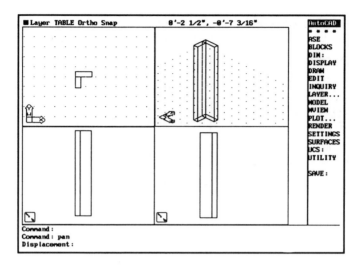

ROUTERING THE TABLE LEG (Solfill)

The table leg is rounded on the outside. The rounding can be simulated in AutoCAD with the Solfill command, short for solids fillet.

1. Start the Solfill command, as follows:

   ```
   Command: solfill
   ```

2. Carefully pick the vertical line that represents the outside edge of the table leg at the following prompt (you may find it easier to use Zoom W to get a close-up view of the outside edge in the lower left viewport):

   ```
   Select edges to be filleted (Press ENTER when done): <pick>
   <Enter>
   1 edges selected.
   ```

3. Specify a radius of a half inch, as follows:

   ```
   Diameter/<Radius> of fillet <0.00>: 1/2
   Phase I - Boundary evaluation begins.
   1 of 12 of Phase I in process.
   Phase II - Tessellation computation begins.
   1 of 7 of Phase II in process.
   Updating the Advanced Modeling Extension database.
   ```

After AutoCAD has finished its many calculations, the fillet appears down the outside of the table leg.

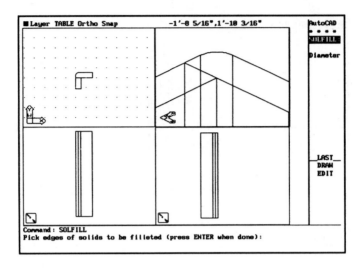

Since you are using solids modelling, you might expect to see a solid-looking table leg on the screen. Instead, you are looking at something that looks like it was fashioned from wires. Indeed, this representation of a 3D drawing is called a "wireframe." The table leg is mathematically solid. In the next hour you take advantage of this fact.

ADDING THREE MORE TABLE LEGS (Move, Array)

With one table leg drawn, you can now move it into position with the Move command, then create the other three legs with the Array command.

1. Using the upper left viewport, move the table leg to the upper left corner with the Move command, as follows:

```
Command: m
MOVE Select objects: <pick upper left viewport> c
First corner: <pick>
Other corner: <pick>
2 found Select objects: <Enter>
Base point or displacement: 0,0
Second point of displacement: -18-1/4,17-1/4
```

The leg disappears and reappears in the upper left corner. If you don't see it reappear, you may have to use the Zoom All command to change the view.

2. Use the Array command to create three more table legs, effortlessly, as follows:

```
Command: array
Select objects: p
2 found Select objects: <Enter>
Rectangular or Polar array (R/P): p
Center point of array: 0,0
Number of items: 4
Angle to fill (+=ccw, -=cw) <360>: 360
Rotate objects as they are copied? <Y> y
```

Having the center of the table at the origin (0,0) makes it a trivial matter to array the legs around the table. Using the Polar option rotates the legs so that the rounded part always faces out. Use the Zoom All command to see the four legs in all four viewports. It's a good idea to save the drawing at this point.

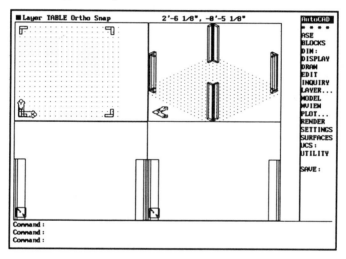

THE TOP AND UNDER-TABLE SUPPORT
(Elev, Regenall, Redrawall)

Repeating the Solbox, Solfill, Move, and Array commands lets you create the tabletop and under-table support bars.

Before drawing the tabletop, move the working elevation up in the z-direction. Until now, you have been (perhaps unknowingly) working at an elevation of 0'-0". When you drew the table legs, the height of 17.25" went from the current working elevation of 0'-0" to 17-1/4". Now you want the tabletop drawn on top of the legs.

1. Thus you use the Elev command to change the working elevation to the top of the table legs, as follows:

```
Command: elev
New current elevation <0'-0">: 17.25
New current thickness <0'-0">: <Enter>
```

You have moved the current elevation from 0'0" to 17-1/4", the distance from the floor that the tabletop begins. Notice how the grid also moves up.

2. Draw the tabletop as a large square sized 36" x 36" x 3/4", as follows:

```
Command: solbox
Corner of box: -18,-18
Cube/Length/<Other corner>: 18,18
Height: 3/4
Phase I - Boundary evaluation begins.
1 of 6 of Phase I in process.
Phase II - Tessellation computation begins.
1 of 6 of Phase II in process.
Updating the Advanced Modeling Extension database.
```

3. If the tabletop does not appear in all four viewports, use the Regenall command to regenerate the drawing in all viewports, as follows:

```
Command: regenall
Regenerating drawing.
```

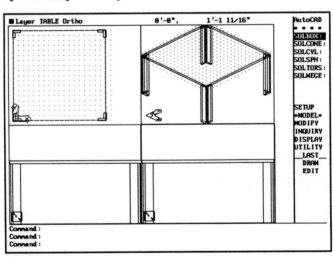

4. Use the Solfill command to round off the top edges of the tabletop, as follows :

```
Command: solfill
```

5. Picking the top edges of the tabletop can be tricky. Look at the upper right viewport (the isometric view) in the following figure to see which lines to pick, shown as the dotted lines.

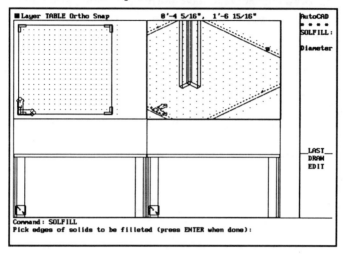

```
Select edges to be filleted (Press ENTER when done): <pick
    four edges> <Enter>
4 edges selected.
Diameter/<Radius> of fillet <0.50> : <Enter>
Phase I - Boundary evaluation begins.
1 of 19 of Phase I in process.
Phase II - Tessellation computation begins.
1 of 12 of Phase II in process.
Updating the Advanced Modeling Extension database.
```

After a long wait, AutoCAD redraws the tabletop with four filleted edges. The following figure shows closeup views of the result.

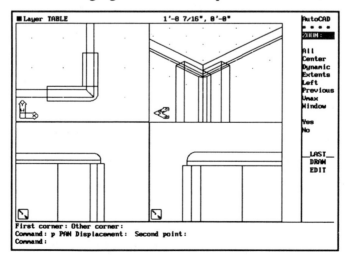

Notice how well AutoCAD handles the intersection of the two filleted edges. There is no cleanup work left for you.

6. If the drawing seems to have portions missing, you can clean up all four viewports at once with the Redrawall command, as follows:

```
Command: redrawall
```

7. With the tabletop drawn, you can add the under-table support bars. The support bars are dimensioned 30"L x 3/4"W x 2- 3/4"H. Like the table legs, you draw one support bar, move it into place, and create three copies. Use the upper left viewport.

```
Command: solbox
Corner of box: 0,0
Cube/Length/<Other corner>: L
Length: 30
Width: 3/4
Height: 2.75
Phase I - Boundary evaluation begins.
1 of 6 of Phase I in process.
Phase II - Tessellation computation begins.
1 of 6 of Phase II in process.
Updating the Advanced Modeling Extension database.
Command: m
MOVE Select objects: L
1 found Select objects: <Enter>
Base point or displacement: 0,0,0
Second point of displacement: -15,-17-7/8,-2.75
Command: array
Select objects: L
1 found Select objects: <Enter>
Rectangular or Polar array (R/P): <P> <Enter>
Center point of array: 0,0
Number of items: 4
Angle to fill (+=ccw, -=cw) <360>: <Enter>
Rotate objects as they are copied? <Y> <Enter>
```

The four support bars drop neatly into place.

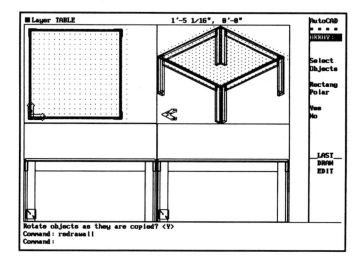

Save the drawing and use the Plot command to print a copy on your printer (see figure below). Warning: AutoCAD does not plot all four viewports; you must first pick the viewport you want plotted.

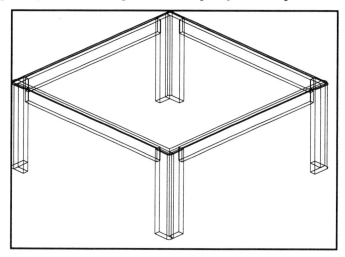

In this hour, you learned a lot about three-dimensional drafting. You created viewports, loaded the Advanced Modelling Extension, and created the table out of simple rectangular boxes. Next hour, you use more solids modelling commands to create and analyze the clips that attach the tabletop to the frame.

HOUR SEVEN

ANALYZING 3D OBJECTS

INTRODUCTION

In the last hour, you learned how to set up AutoCAD for a three-dimensional drawing. You created four viewports with four different views and constructed a coffee table using solids modelling. You saw how a complex shape could be created from simple boxes.

This hour, you learn more about solids modelling. You construct the bracket that holds the tabletop to its frame, analyze the bracket's physical properties, and insert it into the Table drawing as a block.

SETTING UP THE NEW DRAWING

There are 12 small L-shaped brackets that hold the top of the table to the frame. Since the bracket has a symmetrical shape, you only need to draw one leg of one bracket. AutoCAD can draw the second leg for you, as well as the other eleven brackets.

1. Start a new drawing, called Bracket. If you need help with any of these steps, review the beginning of the last hour.
2. Use the Ddunits command to set architectural units with 1/16-inch accuracy.
3. With either the Layer command or the Ddlmodes command, make a new layer called Bracket and color it red.
4. With the Ddrmodes command, set the snap to 1/16", the grid to 1", and turn on the ortho, snap and grid.
5. With the Limits command, set the limits to -2,-2, and 2,2.

6. With the Mvsetup command, create four viewports with the standard engineering views.

7. With the Mspace command, switch to model space.

8. Load AME from the pop-down menu.

MODELLING CYLINDERS (Solcyl)

The drawing environment is now set up for designing the bracket. Each leg of the bracket is 1" long, 5/8" wide, and 1/8" thick.

1. Begin drawing the leg with the Solbox command, as follows:
   ```
   Command: solbox
   Initializing Advanced Modeling Extension.
   ```

2. Start the corner of the box at (0,-1/2) so that the origin of the bracket is at the center edge. The origin point becomes important later in this chapter.
   ```
   Baseplane/Center/<Corner of box>: <0,0,0> 0,-1/2
   Cube/Length/<Other corner>: L
   Length: 1
   Width: 5/8
   Height: 1/8
   ```

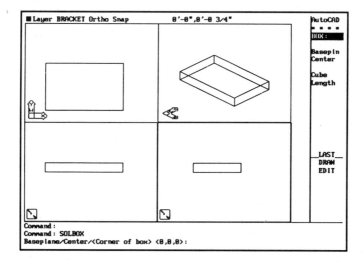

The hole in the bracket is a round opening 1/4" in diameter. Modelling a hole with AME takes two steps: (1) draw a cylinder; (2) remove the material that the cylinder represents. You do this twice: once for the screw hole and once for the rounded end.

3. First draw a construction line with mid object snap to help locate the screw hole, as follows:

```
Command: <pick upper right viewport> line
From point: mid
of <pick bottom left edge of box>
To point: @3/4<0
To point: <Enter>
```

Use the Zoom 3 and Pan commands if you need to see more clearly the objects in the four viewports.

4. To draw the screw hole, use the Solcyl (short for solids cylinder) command, as follows:

```
Command: solcyl
Elliptical/<Center point>: end
of <pick right end of construction line>
Diameter/<Radius>: 1/8
Height of cylinder: 1/8
Phase I - Boundary evaluation begins.
1 of 3 of Phase I in process.
Phase II - Tessellation computation begins.
1 of 3 of Phase II in process.
Updating the Advanced Modeling Extension database.
```

AutoCAD draws in the cylinder shape in place.

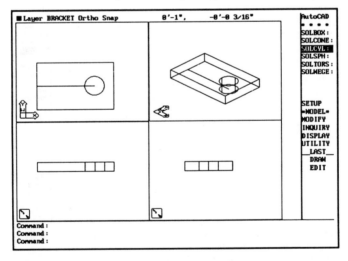

5. The rounded end of the bracket can also be drawn as a cylinder, as follows (use the lower right viewport):

```
Command: solcyl
Elliptical/<Center point>: end
of <pick left end of construction line>
Diameter/<Radius>: 1
Height of cylinder: 1/8
```

The second cylinder should look like the following.

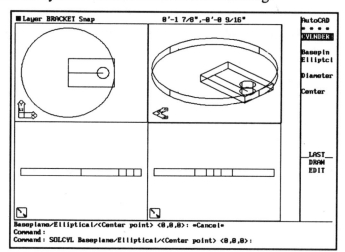

6. Erase the construction line since it is no longer needed:

```
Command: e
ERASE Select objects: <pick line>
Select objects: <Enter>
```

DRILLING HOLES (Solsub, Solint)

In the last chapter, you saw how the AME's Solfill command removed parts of the solid model to create a three-dimensional fillet. To remove the material of the bracket that represents the screw hole and the rounded edge, AME has three other editing commands. These commands use "Boolean logic" to add, subtract, or intersect the volumes common to two or more solid objects.

1. To remove the solid cylinder from the bracket, you use the Solsub (short for solids subtraction) command, as follows:

```
Command: solsub
Source objects...
Select objects: <pick rectangle>
1 selected, 1 found Select objects: <Enter>
1 solid selected.
Objects to subtract from them...
Select objects: <pick small cylinder>
1 selected, 1 found Select objects: <Enter>
1 solid selected.
```

The Solsub command subtracts a solid from another. The picking order is important. If you had picked the cylinder before the box, then you would have been left with a solid cylinder instead of a hole in a box. When AME is finished with its calculations, the drawing looks exactly the same. Since AutoCAD displays the model as a wireframe drawing, a cylinder looks the same, whether it is solid or a hole.

2. To remove most of the cylinder that represents the rounded end, you use the Solint (short for solids intersection) command. That's because the box and the cylinder intersect. Use the Solint command, as follows:

```
Command: solint
Select objects: <pick rectangle>
1 selected, 1 found Select objects: <pick large cylinder>
1 selected, 1 found Select objects: <Enter>
2 solids selected.
```

AutoCAD finds the solid volume common to both the cylinder and the box. When AME has finished its calculations, you should see the leg with a hole and a rounded end.

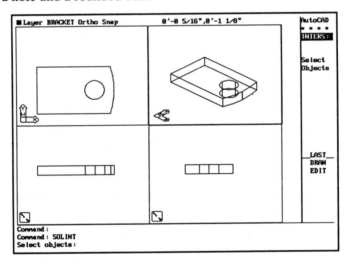

DRAWING THE SECOND LEG (UCS, Solunion)

With one leg of the bracket complete, you can use AutoCAD's editing commands to add the second leg. There are several ways to create a second leg at right angles to the first: (1) the Array command; (2) the Mirror command; (3) the Copy and Rotate commands. The last method is the easiest to use in the complex world of three-dimensional drafting.

114

1. Use the Copy command to create a copy of the leg on top of itself. Place the crossing window around the bracket leg, as follows:

```
Command: copy
Select objects: c
First corner: <pick>
Other corner: <pick>
1 found Select objects: <Enter>
<Base point or displacement>/Multiple: 0,0,0
Second point of displacement: 0,0,0
```

AutoCAD draws a copy of the leg over the top of the original.

2. The Rotate command only works if the current UCS is parallel to the current view. That means you need to use the UCS command, as follows:

```
Command: <pick lower left viewport> ucs
```

3. Use the "v" (short for view) option to orientate the UCS to the current view, as follows:

```
Origin/ZAxis/3point/Entity/View/X/Y/Z/Prev/Restore/
Save/Del/?/<World>: v
Grid too dense to display
```

I find the V option to be the only one of the UCS command's 14 options that I use.

4. Use the Rotate command to change the orientation of the copy by 90 degrees, as follows:

```
Command: rotate
Select objects: L
1 found Select objects: <Enter>
Base point: int
of <pick lower left corner of box>
<Rotation angle>/Reference: 90
```

AutoCAD rotates the copied leg into the up position. Enter **Regenall** to redisplay the original bracket leg.

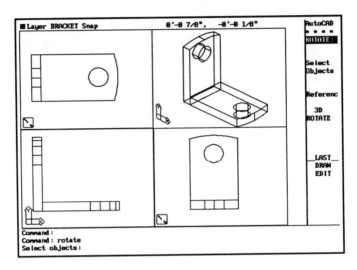

5. Now use the Move command to line up the vertical leg with the horizontal leg, as follows:

```
Command: m
MOVE Select objects: L
1 found Select objects: <Enter>
Base point or displacement: <pick lower left corner of
vertical leg>
Second point of displacement: <pick lower left corner of
horizontal leg>
```

6. With the two legs in place, you use the AME's Solunion (short for solids union) command to join the two legs into a single bracket, as follows:

```
Command: solunion
Select objects: <pick one leg>
1 selected, 1 found Select objects: <pick other leg>
1 selected, 1 found Select objects: <Enter>
Updating solid...
Done.
2 solids selected.
```

Unlike the Solsub command, it makes no difference the order in which you select solids for the union and intersection processes. When AutoCAD finishes its calculations, you should see a single L-shaped bracket with two holes and rounded ends.

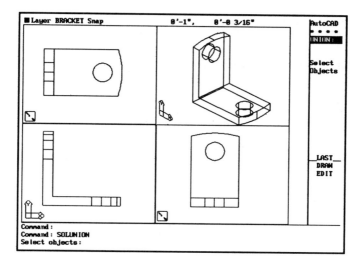

Save the Bracket drawing at this point.

ANALYZING THE BRACKET
(Solarea, Sollist, Ddsolmassp)

A solid model has one important feature over other kinds of three-dimensional models: you can analyze it. AME includes three analysis commands; Autodesk expects third-party vendors to supply other analysis commands. Here you try out AME's three.

1. The Solarea (short for solids area) command finds the surface area of the bracket, as follows:

```
Command: solarea
Select objects: <pick bracket>
1 selected. Select objects: <Enter>
1 solid selected.
Updating the Advanced Modeling Extension database.
Surface meshing of current solid is completed.
Creating block for mesh representation...
Done.
Surface area of solids is 2.889714 sq cm
```

AME determined that the bracket's surface area is about 2.9 square centimeters.

2. The Sollist (short for solids listing) command lists the drawing database information that AutoCAD has stored on the solid model. Try the Sollist command as follows:

```
Command: sollist
Edge/Face/Tree/<Object>: <Enter>
```

117

```
Select objects: <pick bracket>
1 selected, 1 found Select objects: <Enter>
1 solid selected.
```

The Sollist command gives you information on an edge, face, or volume (the Solid option) of the model. Here is the output from the Solid option:

```
Solid type = UNION     Handle = F7
    Component handles:  D1 and B2
    Area = 2.889714
Material = MILD_STEEL
    Representation = WIREFRAME     Shade type = CSG
Rigid motion:
        +1.000000 +0.000000 +0.000000 +0.000000
        +0.000000 +1.000000 +0.000000 +0.000000
        +0.000000 +0.000000 +1.000000 +0.000000
        +0.000000 +0.000000 +0.000000 +1.000000
```

If you hadn't first found the area with Solarea, the Sollist command would have reported, "Area not computed."

3. Here is the information about the CSG tree (short for constructive solid geometry) that links together all the pieces you used to created the bracket:

```
Command: sollist
Edge/Face/Tree/<Solid>: t
Select objects: <pick bracket>
1 selected, 1 found Select objects: <Enter>
1 solid selected.

Object type = UNION     Handle = F7
    Component handles:  D1 and B2
    Area = 2.889714    Material = MILD_STEEL
    Representation = WIREFRAME     Render type = CSG

.... Object type = INTERSECTION     Handle = D1
.... Component handles:  BA and BB
.... Area not computed    Material = MILD_STEEL
.... Representation = WIREFRAME     Render type = CSG
.... Node level = 1

.... Object type = SUBTRACTION     Handle = BA
.... Component handles:  B8 and B9
.... Area not computed    Material = MILD_STEEL
.... Representation = WIREFRAME     Render type = CSG
.... Node level = 2

.... Object type = BOX (1.000000, 0.625000, 0.125000)
        Handle = B8
.... Area not computed    Material = MILD_STEEL
.... Representation = WIREFRAME     Render type = CSG
.... Node level = 3

.... Object type = CYLINDER (0.125000, 0.125000, 0.125000)
        Handle = B9
Press ENTER to continue: <Ctrl>-C
```

Press <Enter> to continue the listing or press <Ctrl>-C to terminate the list.

By keeping track of the constituent parts, AutoCAD can take the model apart again if you decide to use the Undo command.

4. If you are a design engineer, the third inquiry command is of the greatest interest. The Ddsolmassp (short for dynamic dialog solids mass properties) command analyzes the solid model and reports back its mass properties, including its mass, volume, centroid, and moments of inertia. Try it now:

```
Command: ddsolmassp
Select objects: <pick bracket>
1 selected, 1 found Select objects: <Enter>
1 solid selected.
Calculating mass properties.
10 of 81 Mass Phase calculation in process.
```

AME goes through a number of calculations, then displays the following dialog box.

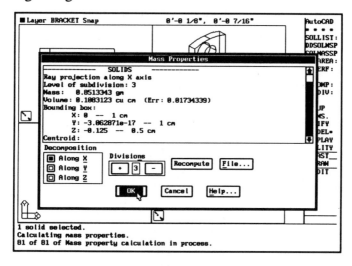

To scroll through all the information, click on the arrows to the right of the listing.

To perform a more accurate calculation, increase the number of divisions from 3 to 8 by clicking on the **+**, then click on **Recompute**.

To save the data to file, click on **Files....** AutoCAD saves the data in a text file with the file extension of MPR (short for mass property report). You will find this report saved on your computer's hard disk with the name BRACKET.MPR in the AutoCAD subdirectory.

INSTALLING THE BRACKETS ON THE TABLE
(Insert *, Copy M)

Now that you have created one bracket, you can install it and eleven more on the underside of the tabletop. Recall that any AutoCAD drawing can be inserted as a block into another AutoCAD drawing.

1. With the Open command, load the Table drawing into AutoCAD.

2. You no longer need the four viewports. Combine them into a single viewport as follows:

```
Command: tilemode
New value for TILEMODE <0>: 1
Regenerating drawing.
Command: zoom all
```

You should now see the top view of the table filling the screen.

3. Spin the table around to view it from the front with the Vpoint (short for viewpoint) command, as follows:

```
Command: vpoint
Rotate/<View point> <0'-1",0'-1",0'-1">: 1,0,0
Regenerating drawing.
```

4. You may find it easier to insert the rather small brackets by zooming in for a closer look. Use the Zoom W command to enlarge the area around the left table leg.

5. Use the Insert * command to bring the Bracket drawing into this drawing, as follows:

```
Command: insert
Block name (or ?): *bracket
Insertion point: <pick any convenient point>
X scale factor <1> / Corner / XYZ: <Enter>
Y scale factor (default=X): <Enter>
Rotation angle <0.0000>: <Enter>
Duplicate definition of block AME_NIL   ignored.
Duplicate definition of block AME_SOL   ignored.
Duplicate definition of block AME_JNK   ignored.
```

The * (asterisk) in front of the drawing name imports the bracket as an "exploded" block. This is important for performing the rendering in Hour 8.

AutoCAD draws the bracket in place, but upside-down.

6. Change the UCS to match the current view, as follows:

```
Command: ucs
Origin/.../<World>: v
```

7. Use the Rotate command to spin the bracket into the correct orientation, as follows:

```
Command: rotate
Select objects: <pick bracket>
4 found Select objects: <Enter>
Base point: <pick anywhere>
<Rotation angle>/Reference: 180
```

8. With the bracket correctly oriented in space, move it into place against the inside of the table in three steps: (1) change the viewpoint to the top view; (2) change the UCS to match the view; (3) move the bracket in place, as follows:

```
Command: vpoint
Rotate/<View point> <0'-1",0'-0",0'-0">: 0,0,0
Regenerating drawing.
Command: ucs
Origin/.../<World>: v
Command: move
Select objects: p
4 found Select objects: <Enter>
Base point or displacement: mid
of <pick left side of bracket>
Second point of displacement: nea of <pick inside of table
    support beam>
```

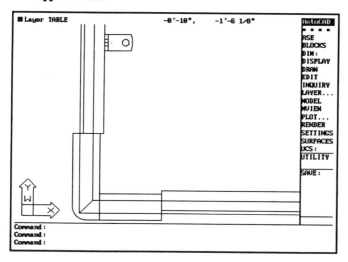

If it helps to make more accurate picks, use zoom window (zw) to get a closer look.

9. The table has 12 brackets: three along each of the four sides. You can use AutoCAD's Copy and Mirror commands to add most of the other brackets, as follows:

```
Command: copy
Select objects: c
First corner: <pick>
Other corner: <pick>
1 found Select objects: <Enter>
```

10. The "m" option allows you to make multiple copies of an object, as follows:

```
<Base point or displacement>/Multiple: M
Base point or displacement: ins
of <pick bracket>
Second point of displacement: mid
of <pick a point on table>
Second point of displacement: nea
of <pick a point on table>
Second point of displacement: <Ctrl>-C
```

Press <Ctrl>-C to terminate the repetitive copying.

11. Now use the Mirror command to create a second set of brackets on the opposite side of the table.

```
Command: mirror
Select objects: <pick three brackets>
Select objects: <Enter>
First point of mirror line: 0,0
Second point: 0,1
Delete old objects? <N> n
```

12. Use the Copy, Rotate (by 90 degrees) Copy M, and Mirror (use midobject snap) commands to insert three brackets at the top and bottom edges of the table.

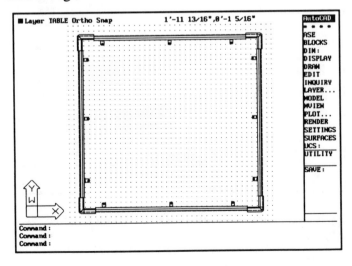

Save the Table drawing and plot the results.

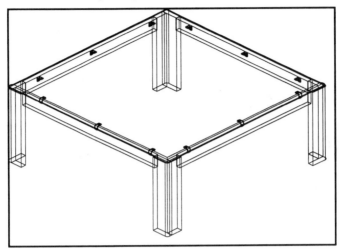

In this hour, you learned more of AutoCAD's solid modelling commands. You joined solid parts together and analyzed the bracket. Next hour, you find out how to make the solid model look more realistic with hidden-line removal, shading, and rendering.

HOUR EIGHT

VIEWING IN THREE DIMENSIONS

INTRODUCTION

In the last hour, you learned more of AutoCAD's solid modelling commands. This final hour, you learn how to make the coffee table look more realistic by removing hidden lines and shading the model of the table.

Note: If your AutoCAD system lacks AME and you were unable to follow along with hours 6 and 7, you can join in this chapter. Load the drawing named HOUR7.DWG from the bonus diskette and follow along.

BEFORE YOU BEGIN (Solmesh)

AutoCAD creates solid models represented as a "wireframe." As you might guess from the term, a wireframe object cannot be shaded or have hidden lines removed. Before you go on, you need to convert the solid model from its wireframe representation into a meshed object. Meshing a solid model means that a mathematical mesh is applied to the surfaces of the model.

1. First, switch to an isometric view of the table if it isn't already like that:

```
Command: vpoint
Rotate/<View point> <0'-0",0'-0",0'-1">: 1,1,1
Regenerating drawing.
```

2. The Solmesh converts a solid model into a meshed object, as follows:

```
Command: solmesh
```

3. If you just loaded the Table drawing into a new AutoCAD session, AME won't have been loaded yet. AutoCAD does this automatically for you:

```
Initializing...
No modeler is loaded yet. Both AME and Region Modeler are
available.
Autoload Region/<AME>: <Enter>
Initializing Advanced Modeling Extension.
```

4. Use All object selection to select the entire table and all 12 brackets, as follows:

```
Select objects: all
36 selected, 36 found
Select objects: <Enter>
Updating solid...
Done.
36 solid selected.
```

The solid model of the coffee table looks exactly the same, but now you can go on to remove the hidden lines.

The drawback to a meshed object is that you can no longer analyze it as a solid model. You turn a meshed object back into a wireframe solid model with the Solwire command.

REMOVING HIDDEN LINES (Hide)

With the solid model converted into an equivalent mesh model, you can get a clearer picture of the three-dimensional coffee table. AutoCAD can remove the lines normally hidden from your view. This process is referred to as "hidden line removal."

1. To remove hidden lines, use the Hide command, as follows:

```
Command: hide
Regenerating drawing.
Removing hidden lines: 5275
```

The process that the Hide command goes through is quite calculation intensive. It will take about one minute for AutoCAD to finish redrawing the coffee table.

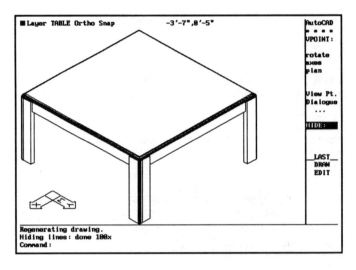

2. To return the hidden lines to view, use the Regen command, as follows:

```
Command: regen
Regenerating drawing.
```

SHADING AND RENDERING (Shade)

The primary purpose of the Shade command is to create quick shaded images of 3D models. There are four different kinds of shading available with the Shade command, as the following table shows:

Value of Shadedge	Shading Style
0	256 colors
1	256 colors—outlined
2	Hidden-line removal
3 (default)	16 colors

To properly display the 256-color shadings, your computer requires a graphics board and device driver capable of displaying 256 colors simultaneously. The shading is less realistic for graphics boards that display only 16 colors.

1. The simple 16-color shading works with almost every graphics board, as follows:

```
Command: shade
Regenerating drawing.
Shading 10% done.
Shading complete.
```

In about the same time as it took to remove hidden lines with the Shade command, the coffee table should reappear looking solid.

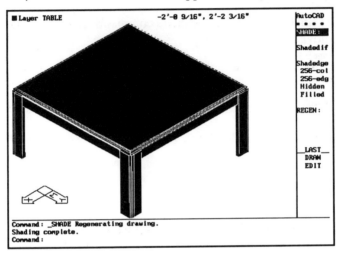

2. Before trying the Shade command again, change the viewpoint to underneath the table, as follows:

```
Command: vpoint
Rotate/<View point> <0'-1",0'-1",0'-1">: -1,-1,-1
Regenerating drawing.
```

Supplying a negative z-coordinate causes AutoCAD to generate a view from "underneath."

3. Zoom in on one of the brackets at the corner of the table.

```
Command: zoom
All/.../<Scale(X/X)>: w
First corner: <pick>
Other corner: <pick>
```

4. If your computer has a graphics board and device driver installed that can display 256 colors, then there are two other ways the Shade command can display shaded images. The first is a 256-color shaded image, which you get by setting Shadedge to 0, as follows:

```
Command: shadedge
New value for SHADEDGE <3>: 0
Command: shade
```

5. The second 256-color method of shading highlights the edges of each face with the background color. This is useful if many faces have the same color.

```
Command: shadedge
New value for SHADEDGE <0>: 1
Command: shade
```

6. The final variation on the Shade command simulates hidden line removal:

```
Command: shadedge
New value for SHADEDGE <1>: 2
Command: shade
```

7. Invoke a regeneration to return the view to show all lines, as follows:

```
Command: regen
Regenerating drawing.
```

PERSPECTIVE VIEWS (Dview)

So far, you have been working with orthographic views. AutoCAD can also display three-dimensional objects in perspective views. This is done with the Dview command (short for dynamic view). The Dview command is possibly the most confusing of AutoCAD's commands. For this reason, you use it here simply to change the view from orthographic to perspective.

1. Begin the Dview command and select the entire table, as follows:

```
Command: dview
Select objects: all
36 found Select objects:
Select objects: <Enter>
```

2. After AutoCAD redraws the table, the Dview command presents a prompt with the following 12 options:

```
CAmera/TArget/Distance/POints/PAn/Zoom/TWist/CLip/
Hide/Off/Undo/<eXit>: d
```

3. Enter "d" to use the distance option, which turns on perspective viewing mode, and enter a camera-to-target distance of eight feet, as follows:

```
New camera/target distance <0'-1 3/4">: 8'
```

4. AutoCAD redraws the coffee table with a one-point perspective view (see the following figure). Note two changes to the screen: (1) the UCS icon has changed to a perspective box to remind you that perspective mode is on; (2) the coordinates disappear from the status line, since coordinate values no longer make sense in a view warped by perspective. In addition, you cannot access the pop-down menus while the Dview command is active.

5. Use the Hide option to remove the hidden lines, as shown in the figure below.

```
CAmera/.../<eXit>: h
Hiding lines: 100% done.
```

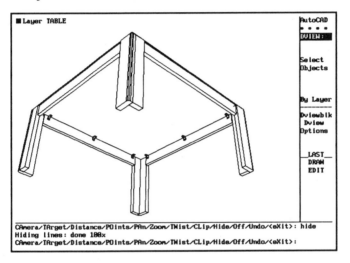

6. Exit the Dview command, as follows:

```
CAmera/.../<eXit>: x
```

7. The irritating thing about perspective mode is that you cannot use the normal Zoom command; instead, you must use the Zoom option of the Dview command. To exit perspective mode, use the Plan command, as follows:

```
Command: plan
<Current UCS>/Ucs/World: <Enter>
Regenerating drawing.
```

The perspective-cube icon is replaced by the UCS icon.

HIGHER-QUALITY RENDERINGS (Render)

In addition to the Shade command, AutoCAD Release 12 includes a medium-quality rendering module called the AutoCAD Visualization Extension (or Render, for short). Prior to Release 12, Render was an extra-cost add-on product called AutoShade.

Render works in three modes, which I call simple, advanced, and RenderMan. The simple mode is much like the Shade command. You simply type the Render command and AutoCAD renders the 3D drawing using a light source that appears to be located at your eye. In advanced mode, you can specify the type and positioning of many lights, the color and shininess of the objects' surfaces, and a number of rendering types. RenderMan is an extra-cost optional add-on that lets you create photo-realistic renderings of 3D AutoCAD drawings.

Before being able to use Render at all, your computer must have a graphics board supported by an AutoCAD rendering driver. Release 12 supports rendering on several graphics boards compatible with 8514, XGA, Targa, and VESA-compliant SuperVGA graphics boards, but not plain VGA boards.

1. Before using Render for the first time, you must configure Render for your graphics board. This happens automatically when you attempt to use Render, as follows:

```
Command: render
Initializing...
Initializing AVE Render...
Please reconfigure RENDER,
Press RETURN to continue: <Enter>

AVE_RENDER is not yet configured.
Select rendering display device:
1. AutoCAD's configured P386 ADI combined display/rendering
driver
2. P386 Autodesk Device Interface rendering driver
3. None (Null rendering device)
Rendering selection <1>: <Enter>
```

2. Another advantage of Render over the Shade command is that it lets you create printouts of the rendered drawings. However, you need to have a hardcopy device supplied with a device driver specific to Render. If you have none, then select option 1, as follows:

```
Select rendering hard copy device:
1.  None (Null rendering device)
2.  P386 Autodesk Device Interface rendering driver
3.  Rendering file (256 color map)
```

```
4.  Rendering file (continuous color)
Rendering hard copy selection <1>: <Enter>
```

3. With Render configured for your computer's graphics board (and, optionally, the hardcopy device), AutoCAD renders the coffee table.

PLOTTING HIDDEN LINE DRAWINGS

Now that you have created all these beautiful views of your expertly crafted coffee table, how do you create a hardcopy of them? AutoCAD Release 12 provides a number of ways.

You can plot the drawing to your printer or save it in a number of raster formats, such as an SLD slide, in PCX or in TIFF format. Once in a raster format, you can import the image into a paint program (such as Microsoft Paintbrush) or a word processor (such as WordPerfect).

To create a hidden line plot, you can't just start the Plot command from a view that has the hidden lines removed. Instead, you need to set the Plot command for hidden line removal. That's because the Plot command performs a more accurate removal of hidden lines since the printer has a higher resolution than the video display.

1. Start the Plot command, as follows:
   Command: **plot**

2. When the Plot Configuration dialog box appears, look for the Additional Parameters section. Click on the box next to **Hide Lines**.

3. Now you can go ahead and plot the drawing as before. AutoCAD regenerates the plot, removes the hidden lines, and outputs the data to the printer.

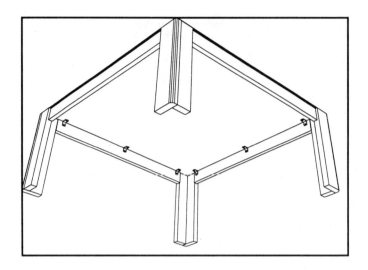

CAPTURING SHADED IMAGES (Saveimg, Replay, MSlide, VSlide)

Here are several ways to capture AutoCAD's shaded and rendered images.

Renderings　For the Render command, you can capture the screen image with the Saveimg (short for save image) command. Saveimg saves the rendering in one of four raster formats: Targa TGA, GIF, TIFF, and RND. Of the four, TIFF is the most universally accepted.

1. Start the Saveimg command, as follows:

   Command: **saveimg**

AutoCAD displays the Save Image dialog box. Click on the box next to **TIFF.**

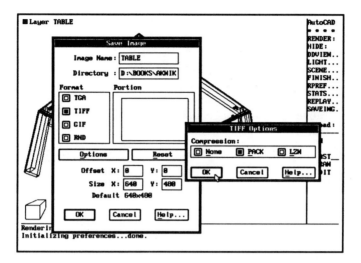

2. Since color TIFF files can get very large (in excess of 1MB), there are two compression options available. Click on the **Options** button.

3. When the TIFF Options dialog box appears, choose either the **PACK** or **LZW** compression options. Packbits is best for monochrome images, while LZW is best for color images.

4. Click on the **OK** button to return to the Save Image dialog box.

5. Click on the **OK** button to save the image to disk.

6. To view the saved TIFF file, use the Replay command.

SLD Files For the Shade command, you can capture the screen image with the MSlide (short for make slide) command. MSlide captures the graphics portion of the screen (it does not capture the three text areas) and saves the image on the hard disk as an SLD (short for slide) file.

1. Shade the coffee table again with the Shade command.

2. Use the MSlide command, as follows:
```
Command: mslide
Slide file <table>: <Enter>
```

AutoCAD saves the shaded image as a file called TABLE.SLD on the computer's hard disk. This file can be read into many desktop publishing programs, including Ventura Publisher and WordPerfect.

3. Use the Regen command to remove the shaded image:
```
Command: regen
Regenerating drawing.
```

4. View slide files with the VSlide command, as follows:

```
Command: vslide
Slide file <table>: <Enter>
```

The image of the shaded table reappears on the screen. You cannot edit or change the slide image in any way.

5. To remove the slide image, use the Redraw command, as follows:

```
Command: redraw
```

The shaded image is replaced with the wireframe image.

Raster Plots   You can configure the Plot command for any of nearly a dozen raster output files for DOS and Unix systems:

- Adobe EPSF (encapsulated PostScript image file)
- Aldus-Microsoft TIFF (tagged image file format)
- Amiga IFF/ILBM (image file format)
- CCITT G3 (fax group 3 encoding)
- CompuServe GIF (graphics interchange format)
- Jef Pskanzer PBM (portable bitmap)
- Microsoft Windows BMP (bitmap)
- NTSC FITS (flexible image transfer system)
- Sun Rasterfile
- TrueVision TGA (targa)
- X Windows XWD (screen dump)
- Z-Soft PCX (paintbrush format)

Screen Grabs   Capture the screen with screen capture software, available with most paint programs and desktop publishing programs. Import the screen capture image into the paint or dtp program, which can print the image. For this book, I used the <Print Screen> key while running AutoCAD in Windows, then pasted the Clipboard image into Image-In Color Professional.

Camera   Take a picture of the screen with your camera mounted on a tripod for a steady image. Use a 100mm lens to minimize screen curvature. In a darkened room to eliminate glare, take the pictures as follows:

1. Set a slow shutter speed (1/30 sec or less) to eliminate screen blanking.
2. Set a small aperture (f1/16) to ensure the picture is in focus.

3. Bias the exposure (experiment with +1 or +2) to reduce overexposure.

In this last hour, you learned several different ways to display three-dimensional drawings, including hidden line removal and shading. By working through to the end of this book, you have learned the commands you use most often with AutoCAD.

APPENDIX

INSTALLING AND CONFIGURING AUTOCAD

INTRODUCTION

AutoCAD is a very large computer program that works with many kinds of computers and hundreds of different peripherals. Autodesk hopes to have AutoCAD Release 12 running on the following computers and operating systems:

- Intel 80386- and 80486-based computers running DOS
- Intel-based computers running Windows v3.x and NT
- Sun 680x0-based computers running SunView SunOS
- Sun SPARCstation-based computers running SunView SunOS
- DEC VAXstation computers running VMS
- Macintosh-compatible computers
- Silicon Graphics Indigo computer running Unix
- IBM RS/6000 computers running A/IX

There are two things you must do before you can use AutoCAD for computer-aided drafting: (1) install the software; (2) configure the program. This appendix shows you how to install the AutoCAD software and configure the program for a typical hardware setup.

INSTALLING AUTOCAD RELEASE 12

The AutoCAD diskette "Executables 1" contains an installation program that copies the files from the distribution diskettes onto your computer's hard disk. Since the files on the distribution diskettes are stored in compressed format, you cannot copy the files to the computer yourself. The CD-ROM disk included in the Release 12 package contains bonus material, not the AutoCAD program.

Necessary Equipment   Before installing AutoCAD, check that your computer has the hardware required to run Release 12. If you have AutoCAD Release 12 for Extended DOS, your computer must be an IBM-compatible that uses an Intel 80386-compatible CPU.

The computer must have an IBM-compatible 5-1/4" 1.2MB or 3-1/2" 720KB floppy disk to read the AutoCAD diskettes and at least 23MB of space free on the hard disk to store the AutoCAD program. The computer must be equipped with a graphics board that is supplied with an ADI (Autodesk Device Interface) device driver or is compatible with one of the following standards:

- Hercules monochrome graphics
- IBM EGA (enhanced graphics adapter)
- IBM VGA (video graphics array), Super VGA or VESA-compatible
- IBM 8514/A
- IBM XGA (extended graphics array)

A math chip is required in 386- and 486SX-based computers.

Optional Equipment   It doesn't matter if the monitor displays monochrome or color. A mouse (for controlling the cursor) and printer (for plotting out your drawings) are optional but highly desirable.

Installation   Release 12 comes with an installation program that copies the contents of the AutoCAD diskettes onto the computer's hard drive for you.

1. Before you begin the Install program, check with the DOS Dir command that your computer's hard disk has at least 23MB of free space, as follows:

```
C:\> dir
 Volume in drive C is THIS
 Directory of  C:\
AMY           <DIR>        9-12-90    7:24p
DOS           <DIR>        9-12-90    7:17p
MIDI          <DIR>        9-12-90    7:23p
MODEM         <DIR>        1-14-91    7:35p
PCTOOLS       <DIR>        9-12-90    7:21p
EXCEL         <DIR>        9-12-92    7:20p
WP            <DIR>        9-12-90    7:18p
AUTOEXEC BAT       852     6-28-91   12:29a
CONFIG   SYS       247     6-11-91   10:35a
MIRROR   FIL     50688     6-30-91    3:41p
WP       BAT        47     6-19-91    4:45p
    45 File(s)    25484544 bytes free
```

This C: drive has about 25MB of free disk space. If your computer has more than one hard drive, check all drives. For example, to check the second hard drive, type:

```
C:\>: dir d:
 Volume in drive D is THAT
 Directory of  D:\
USTN          <DIR>        6-04-91    8:28a
CADD6         <DIR>       10-23-90    9:23p
WINDOWS       <DIR>        8-27-90   11:04p
MIRROR   FIL     48640     6-30-91    3:41p
PCTRACKR DEL     36768     6-29-91   11:30a
MIRROR   BAK     48640     6-30-91    9:28a
    10 File(s)    34435072 bytes free
```

The D: drive on this computer has about 34MB of free disk space. Install AutoCAD on the drive with the most free disk space, the D: drive in this case. Don't install AutoCAD at all unless one hard drive has at least 23MB free disk space.

2. Run the Install program by inserting AutoCAD diskette #1 called "Executables 1" into the floppy drive, close the door, and type:
```
C:\> a:install
```

The Install program displays the following screen.

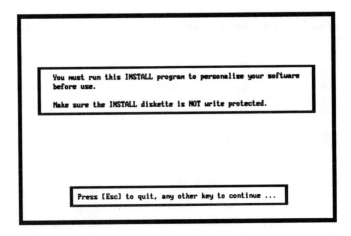

3. The Install program asks you to type your name, company name, dealer name, and dealer telephone number. This information is added to AutoCAD, personalizing the program for you.

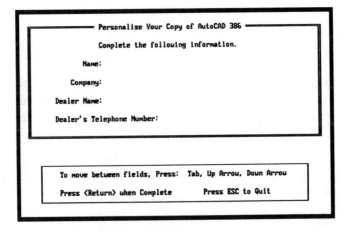

4. After you enter the information, Install asks you for confirmation since the data is permanently written to the AutoCAD file.

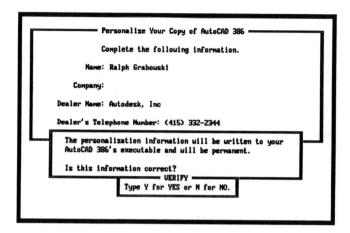

5. Now it's decision time. The Install program can install all of AutoCAD's files or just some of them. If you are short on disk space, then you may want to install only the AutoCAD 386 Executable/Support files. I recommend installing the files marked with YES below:

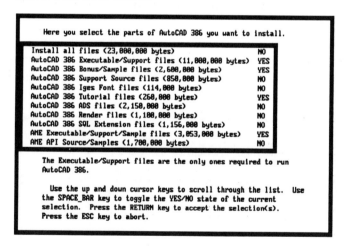

The screen displaying installation options can be confusing to use. Here are the keys to press on the keyboard:

- Use the cursor keys to move the reverse-video bar down and up.
- Use the Spacebar to change NO to YES or back to NO.
- When finished, press the <Enter> key.

The Install program confirms your selections and then begins copying files from the AutoCAD diskette to the hard disk.

6. Next, the Install program asks you on which hard drive you want AutoCAD installed. If your computer has one hard drive, then the only answer is C:. If your computer has more than one hard drive, you have a choice; choose the drive with the most free space.

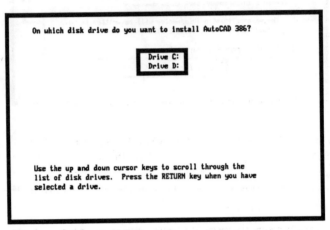

7. The Install program also needs to know in which subdirectory to install AutoCAD. Most likely, you will use the name supplied as the default, ACAD. If the directory doesn't exist, the Install program creates it for you.

8. You also have the option of specifying the subdirectory name for AutoCAD's support files, which include menu files, font files, and hatch pattern files. If you are running more than one version of AutoCAD, such as Release 12 for DOS and Release 11 for Windows, then you will want a common support subdirectory.

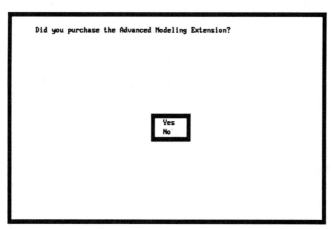

```
Here you specify the name of the directory where AutoCAD 386
support files will be installed.  By default, the name of this
directory is:
  \ACAD\SUPPORT

The program locates it below the root directory of the disk
drive you selected.  If you have no preference, choose the
default by pressing the RETURN key.

To change the directory name, backspace over the directory name
and type a new name.  Press the RETURN key when you have finished
typing the name.



┌──────────── Support files subdirectory ? ────────────┐
│ \ACAD\SUPPORT                                          │
```

9. If you paid for the optional AME solids modelling module, then the Install program will install its files if you answer yes:

```
Did you purchase the Advanced Modeling Extension?




                    ┌─────┐
                    │ Yes │
                    │ No  │
                    └─────┘
```

10. Install then proceeds to copy files from the diskette onto your computer's hard drive. When Install has copied all files from a diskette, the program prompts you to install the next AutoCAD diskette.

```
Installing AutoCAD 386 - Please Wait . . .
     Reading: A:\inst_en.xxx
     Writing: D:\ACAD\inst_en.xxx
     Reading: A:\ACAD.PT1
     Writing: D:\ACAD\ACAD.EXE
     Reading: A:\ACAD1.MID
     Writing: D:\ACAD\ACAD1.MID




        ─────── Press any key to continue ───────
        Please place the Release Disk labeled "Executables 2"
        in drive A:
        Press the ESC key to abort, any other key to continue...
```

11. After all AutoCAD diskettes are copied onto the hard drive, the Install program suggests some changes to the CONFIG.SYS file. The changes help AutoCAD operate faster. Answer Y (for yes) and Install makes the change for you.

12. Similarly, the Install program creates a batch file, called ACADR12.BAT, that helps you start AutoCAD. Answer Y to have Install create the batch file.

The following ACAD12.BAT file, which I use, is a more complete version than the one created by Install.

```
set
acad=c:\acad;c:\acad\support;c:\acad\sample;c:\acad\fonts
set acadcfg=c:\acad
set acaddrv=c:\acad\drv
set avecfg=c:\acad
set asetut=c:\acad\tutorial\dbf
set rdpadi=c:\acad\drv\rchadi42.cfg
c:\acad\acad %1 %2 %3
```

In addition to setting more paths, it also points to the subdirectory where the rendering configuration file is located (avecfg), the SQL database tutorial subdirectory (asetut), and the external rendering device driver (rdpadi).

13. The Install program is now finished. Remove the last AutoCAD diskette from the floppy drive and store all the diskettes in a safe place (like your safety deposit box).

14. Start AutoCAD using the batch file created by Install, as follows:

```
C:> acadr12
```

CONFIGURING AUTOCAD

When you start AutoCAD for the first time, the program reports that it isn't configured, as follows:

```
              A U T O C A D (R)
Copyright (c) 1982-92 Autodesk, Inc.  All Rights Reserved.
Release 12 (6/21/92) 386 DOS Extender
Serial Number:  117-10000000
Licensed to:    Ralph Grabowski
Obtained from:  Autodesk, Inc - (415) 332-2344

AutoCAD is not yet configured.
Searching for files.  Please wait.
```

AutoCAD leads you through the steps required to make the program work with your computer's graphics board, mouse or digitizer (called an input device), plotter or printer (called output devices).

I assume that your computer uses the following peripherals:

- a VGA-compatible graphics board
- a Microsoft Mouse-compatible mouse
- an HP LaserJet III-compatible laser printer

If your computer's equipment list differs, don't panic! The configuration questions are very similar for different brand names within product groups.

CONFIGURING THE GRAPHICS BOARD

AutoCAD first asks you to tell it which graphics board is installed in your computer, as follows:

```
              A U T O C A D (R)
Copyright (c) 1982-92 Autodesk, Inc.  All Rights Reserved.
Release 12 (6/21/92) 386 DOS Extender
Serial Number:  117-10000000
Licensed to:    Ralph Grabowski
Obtained from:  Autodesk, Inc - (415) 332-2344

Available video displays:
   1.  Null display
   2.  8514/A ADI 4.2 Display and Rendering - By Panacea for
       Autodesk
   3.  ADI display v4.0
   4.  ADI display v4.1
   5.  Compaq Portable III Plasma Display <obsolete>
   6.  Hercules Graphics Card <obsolete>
   7.  IBM Enhanced Graphics Adapter <obsolete>
   8.  IBM Video Graphics Array ADI 4.2 - by Autodesk
   9.  SVADI Super VGA ADI 4.2 - by Autodesk
```

```
10.  Targa+ ADI v4.2 Display and Rendering - by Autodesk
11.  VESA Super VGA ADI v4.2 Display and Rendering - by
     Autodesk
12.  XGA ADI 4.2 Display and Rendering - By Panacea for
     Autodesk
Select device number or ? to repeat list <1>: 8
```

The "null display" lets you use AutoCAD without a graphics board installed, such as just for plotting. "Obsolete" drivers work with Release 12 but are not supported by Autodesk if they don't work properly.

1. If your computer has a VGA board installed, type "8" to select the VGA display.

2. AutoCAD asks you four questions, each of which you should answer with the default, as follows:

```
Do you want to do detailed configuration of IBM VGA's
display
features? <N> <Enter>
If you have previously measured the height and width of
a "square" on your graphics screen, you may use these
measurements to correct the aspect ratio.
Would you like to do so? <N> <Enter>

Do you want a status line? <Y> y
Do you want a command prompt area? <Y> y
Do you want a screen menu area? <Y> y
```

The detailed configuration is a complicated process, which you can return to later with the Config command.

You have configured AutoCAD for your computer's graphics board. Next, you configure AutoCAD for your computer's input device.

CONFIGURING THE INPUT DEVICE

AutoCAD can use a mouse or a digitizing tablet:

```
Available digitizers:
  1.  None
  2.  ADI digitizer (Real Mode)
  3.  Calcomp 2500 and 9100 Series ADI 4.2 - by Autodesk
  4.  GTCO Digi-Pad (Types 5 & 5A) <obsolete> ADI 4.2
  5.  Hitachi HICOMSCAN HDG Series ADI 4.2 - by Autodesk
  6.  Kurta IS/1, Series I <obsolete> ADI 4.2 - by Autodesk
  7.  Kurta XLC, Series II and III <obsolete>, IS/3 ADI 4.2
  8.  Logitech Logimouse ADI 4.2 - by Autodesk
  9.  Microsoft Mouse Driver ADI 4.2 - by Autodesk
 10.  Numonics 2200 <obsolete> ADI 4.2 - by Autodesk
```

```
     11.  Summagraphics MM Series v2.0, ADI 4.2 - by Autodesk
     12.  Summagraphics MicroGrid v1.0 (Series II or later)
              ADI 4.2
Select device number or ? to repeat list <1>: 9
```

1. Most mice are compatible with the Microsoft Mouse, even if they are manufactured by Logitech. Type "9" if you use a mouse. If you have a digitizing tablet attached to your computer, then it is most likely compatible with the Summagraphics MM Series.

2. There is only one additional question AutoCAD asks about the mouse:

```
Supported model:
     1.  Microsoft Mouse
One choice, selection is automatic.
Do you want to adjust the mouse scaling parameters? <N>
     <Enter>
```

Answer "N" for now, since the default scaling parameters are adequate.

AutoCAD is now configured for the graphics board and input device.

CONFIGURING THE PRINTER AND PLOTTER

I assume that you have an HP-compatible laser printer attached to your computer; the questions for configuring a pen plotter are similar. The list of plotters and printers supported by Release 12 is long:

```
Available plotters:
     1.  None
     2.  ADI plotter or printer (installed - pre v4.1)
     3.  AutoCAD file output formats (pre 4.1) - by Autodesk
     4.  CalComp ColorMaster Plotters ADI 4.2 - by Autodesk
     5.  CalComp DrawingMaster Plotters ADI 4.2 - by Autodesk
     6.  CalComp Electrostatic Plotters ADI 4.2 - by Autodesk
     7.  CalComp Pen Plotters ADI 4.2 - by Autodesk
     8.  Canon Laser Printer ADI 4.2 - by Autodesk
     9.  Epson printers ADI 4.2 - by Autodesk
    10.  Hewlett-Packard (HP-GL) ADI 4.2 - by Autodesk
    11.  Hewlett-Packard (HP-GL/2) ADI 4.2 - by Autodesk
    12.  Hewlett-Packard (PCL) LaserJet ADI 4.2 - by Autodesk
    13.  Hewlett-Packard (PCL) PaintJet XL ADI 4.2 - by
              Autodesk
    14.  Houston Instrument ADI 4.2 - by Autodesk
    15.  IBM 7300 Series ADI 4.2 - by Autodesk
    16.  IBM Graphics Printer <obsolete> ADI 4.2 - by Autodesk
    17.  IBM Proprinter ADI 4.2 - by Autodesk
    18.  JDL 750 & 750E <obsolete> ADI 4.2 - by Autodesk
    19.  NEC Pinwriter P5/P5XL/P9XL <obsolete> ADI 4.2
    20.  PostScript device ADI 4.2 - by Autodesk
    21.  Raster file export ADI 4.2 - by Autodesk
Select device number or ? to repeat list <1>: 12
```

1. Select option 12 if you have an HP LaserJet-compatible laser printer.

If you do not see the name of your printer or plotter listed, it may well be compatible with one or more in the list. For example, most pen and thermal plotters are compatible with #10 HPGL, while most dot-matrix printers are compatible with #9 or #17, Epson or IBM Proprinter. Naturally, all PostScript printers are compatible with #20.

If don't have an output device, select #1 or #21; the latter option lets you create raster files of drawings in PCX, TIFF, and other common formats.

If you have more than one output device, you can configure for the additional devices later.

2. AutoCAD asks which specific LaserJet model your computer uses:

```
Supported models:
    1.  HP LaserJet
    2.  HP LaserJet Plus
    3.  HP LaserJet II
    4.  HP LaserJet III
    5.  HP LaserJet w/ 2 Mbytes
    6.  HP LaserJet II w/ 1.5 Mbytes
    7.  HP LaserJet III w/ 1 Mbyte
Enter selection, 1 to 7 <1>: 7
```

Select option #7 if you haven't added any memory to the LaserJet III; if the LaserJet III has more than 1MB of memory, select option #4.

3. Next, AutoCAD asks a number of questions related to the operation of the LaserJet. Almost all LaserJets are connected to the computer via the parallel port.

```
Is your plotter connected to a <S>erial, or <P>arallel
port?<P> p
```

4. All LaserJets have the Letter-size paper tray.

```
Paper trays:
------------
    1.  Manual Feed
    2.  Letter
    3.  A4 Sheet
    4.  Legal
Select paper tray currently installed, 1 to 4 <2>: <Enter>
```

5. Selecting a resolution involves deciding on the trade-off between speed and quality. A plot made at 300dpi looks very nice but takes ten times longer than a 75dpi plot. If you use the LaserJet mainly

for quick check plots, then 150dpi is a good trade-off; for presentation plots, choose 300dpi.

```
Possible resolutions (dots/inch):
    1.  75
    2. 100
    3. 150
    4. 300
Select desired resolution, 1 to 4 <4>: <Enter>
```

If the LaserJet III has only 1MB memory, it cannot print the entire drawing at 300dpi on the full sheet of paper. Part of the plot may get cut off.

6. Once AutoCAD has sent a drawing to the LaserJet, the plot information is stored in the printer's memory. The printer can then make additional copies at a rate of eight per minute, acting like a Xerox copier. Sometimes this is useful; most times it is not:

```
How many copies of the plot would you like, 1 to 99 <1>:
    <Enter>
```

7. To make more room for the plot in the printer's memory, AutoCAD can instruct the LaserJet to erase other things stored in memory, such as downloaded fonts and macros. This does not erase the built-in fonts the printer comes with.

```
Would you like to delete all downloaded fonts and macros?
    <N> <Enter>
```

8. Next, AutoCAD searches your computer system to look for all ports the printer could connect to, as follows:

```
Connects to Parallel Printer port.
Standard ports are:
    LPT1
    LPT2
Enter port name, or address in hexadecimal <LPT1>: <Enter>
```

Type in the name of the parallel port that the LaserJet is attached to. If your computer has an unusual printer port setup, you instead type in the port's hexadecimal address. For example, the hex address for parallel port 1 is 0378.

9. Finally, AutoCAD reports the default values of plotting parameters that are best changed during the Plot command:

```
Plot will NOT be written to a selected file
Sizes are in Inches and the style is portrait
Plot origin is at (0.00,0.00)
Plotting area is 8.00 wide by 10.50 high (MAX size)
Plot is NOT rotated
Hidden lines will NOT be removed
```

```
Plot will be scaled to fit available area
Do you want to change anything? (No/Yes/File) <N>: <Enter>
```

Choosing the File option lets you save the configuration information to a file on disk.

You have configured AutoCAD for the graphics board, mouse, and dot-matrix printer. AutoCAD has a few more questions before you are done.

FINAL CONFIGURATION QUESTIONS

Since AutoCAD can be used on a network, it needs to know how to identify you on the network. You must answer the following questions, even if your computer is not on a network:

1. The "login name" is the name by which AutoCAD identifies you to others on a network. You can use the default name, which AutoCAD generates from the personalization information.

```
Login Name:
Enter default login name or . for none <Ralph Grabowski>:
    <Enter>
```

If you enter a period (.) for no default login name, AutoCAD will prompt you for a login name each time you start AutoCAD.

2. You are probably *not* using AutoCAD on a network. Thus, you do not need to change the server authorization information, as follows:

```
Server authorization:
Your current server authorization is 00000000
The maximum number of users for this package is  1
The AutoCAD executable resides in a read/write directory.
WARNING: This information should only be changed while no
other users are currently executing the program.
Do you wish to change it? <N> n
```

Server authorization prevents more than the authorized number of people using AutoCAD on the network.

3. Similarly, you do *not* want to enable file locking, as follows:

```
Do you wish to enable file-locking? <Y> n
```

File locking prevents more than one person using the same drawing file at one time. Since you are the only person using this copy of AutoCAD, you do not need file locking.

4. You have now completed configuring AutoCAD for your computer system. AutoCAD summarized the configuration, as follows:

```
Current AutoCAD configuration

Video display:      IBM Video Graphics Array ADI 4.2
IBM VGA v1.8d (21jun92). Universal Super VGA ADI
   (Display/Render)
DOS Protected Mode ADI 4.2 Driver for AutoCAD.
Config file is D:\ACAD\DRV\SVADI.CFG
Configured for: IBM Video Graphics Array.  Text font: 8x16.
Display - 640x480 in 16 colors on Light background.
Rendering - 320x200 in 256 colors.
Version: A.1.18

Digitizer:          Microsoft Mouse Driver ADI 4.2 - by
                    Autodesk
                    Microsoft Mouse
Version: A.1.18

Plotter:            Hewlett-Packard (PCL) LaserJet ADI 4.2
                    HP LaserJet III w/ 1 Mbyte
Port: Parallel Printer LPT1 at address 378 (hex)
Version: A.1.18

Press RETURN to continue:
```

5. AutoCAD displays the configuration menu, as follows:

```
Configuration menu
    0.  Exit to Main Menu
    1.  Show current configuration
    2.  Allow detailed configuration

    3.  Configure video display
    4.  Configure digitizer
    5.  Configure plotter
    6.  Configure system console
    7.  Configure operating parameters
Enter selection <0>: 0
```

If you have more plotters to configure, select option 5 and AutoCAD leads you through the plotter configuration sequence until you have added all plotters.

Enter "0" to leave AutoCAD's configuration menu.

6. AutoCAD saves the configuration information (in a file called ACAD.CFG) when you answer "Y" to the following question:

```
If you answer N to the following question, all configuration
changes you have just made will be discarded.
Keep configuration changes? <Y> y
```

7. Finally, AutoCAD displays the Drawing Editor screen. From now on, the graphics screen is the first thing you see when you start AutoCAD. If you need to change AutoCAD's configuration, use the Config command, as follows:

```
Command: config
```

As an alternative, you can start AutoCAD with the -r (short for reconfigure) switch at the DOS prompt, as follows:

```
C:\> acad -r
```

Both actions put you into the configuration menu.

8. You can now start with the lesson in Hour 1 or exit AutoCAD with the Quit command, as follows:

```
Command: quit
End AutoCAD.
C:\>
```

In this appendix, you found out about the computer equipment necessary to run AutoCAD. You learned how to install AutoCAD Release 12 and went through the steps of configuring AutoCAD for your computer's peripherals. You can now go on to the first chapter, Setting Up the Drawing, where you learn how to set up AutoCAD for your first drawing.

Index

AutoCAD commands are shown in **bold**